Richard Baxter

The Divine Appointment of the Lords Day Proved

Richard Baxter

The Divine Appointment of the Lords Day Proved

ISBN/EAN: 9783337289966

Printed in Europe, USA, Canada, Australia, Japan

Cover: Foto ©Lupo / pixelio.de

More available books at **www.hansebooks.com**

THE
Divine Appointment
OF THE
Lords Day

Proved: As a separated Day for Holy Worship; especially in the Church Assemblies. And consequently the *Cessation* of the *Seventh day Sabbath*.

Written for the satisfaction of some Religious Persons who are lately drawn into Error or doubting in both these Points.

Robert Steed By *Richard Baxter*. *his book*

Rev. 1. 10. *I was in the Spirit on the Lords Day.*
Col. 2. 16, 17. *Let no man judge you in Meat, or in Drink, or in respect of an Holy day, (or Feast) or of the New Moon, or Sabbaths, which are a shadow of things to come, but the Body is of Christ.*

LONDON,
Printed for *Nevil Simmons*, at the three Crowns near *Holborn* Conduit. 1671.

THE PREFACE.

Reader,

F thou think this Treatise both *superfluous* and *Defective*, when so many larger have better done the work already, I shall not at all gainsay the latter, nor much the former. The reason of my writing it was the necessity and request of some very upright Godly persons, who are lately faln into doubt or Errour, in point of the Sabbath day, conceiving that because the fourth Commandment was Written in Stone,

The Preface.

it is wholly unchangeable, and consequently the seventh day Sabbath in force, and that the Lords day is not a Day separated by God to holy Worship. I knew that there was enough written on this Subject long agoe; But, 1. Much of it is in Latine; 2. Some Writings which prove the abrogation of the Jewish Sabbath, do withal treat so loosly of the Lords day, as that they require a Confutation in the latter as well as a commendation for the former. 3. Some are so large that the persons that I write for will hardly be brought to read them. 4. Most go upon those grounds, which I take to be less clear; and build so much more than I can do on the fourth Commandment and on many passages of the old Testament, and plead so much for the old Sabbatical notion and rest, that I fear this is the chief occasion of many

many peoples Errours; who when they find themselves in a wood of difficulties, and nothing plain and convincing that is pleaded with them, do therefore think it safest to stick to the old Jewish Sabbath The friends and acquaintance of some of these persons importuning me, to take the plainest and nearest way to satisfie such honest doubters, I have here done it according to my judgement: not contending against any that go another way to work, but thinking my self that this is very clear and satisfactory; *viz.* to prove, 1. That Christ did Commission his Apostles to Teach us all things which he commanded, and to settle Orders in his Church, 2. And that he gave them his spirit to enable them to do all this Infallibly, by bringing all his words to their remembrance, and by leading them into all truth. 3. And that his Apostles by by this spirit did *de facto* separate the Lords day, for holy Worship, especially in Church-Assemblies, and declared the cessation of the Jewish Sabbaths. 4. And that as this change had the very same Author as the Holy Scriptures (the Holy Ghost in the Apostles) so that *fact* hath the same kind of proof, that we have of the Canon and the integrity and uncorruptness of the particular Scripture Books and Texts: And that, if so much Scripture as mencioneth the keeping of the Lords day, expounded by the Concent, and Practice of the Universal Church from the dayes of the Apostles, (all keeping this day as holy, without the dissent of any one Sect, or single person that I remember to have read of,) I say if all this History will not fully prove the point of fact, that this day was kept in the Apostles times, and consequently is Canonical, and uncorrupted; nor can we think that any thing in the world, that is past, can have Historical proof.

I have been put to say somewhat particularly out of Antiquity for this evidence of the fact, because it is that which I lay the greatest stress upon. But I have not done it so largely as might be done, 1. Because I would not lose the unlearned Reader in a Wood of History, nor overwhelm him instead of edifying him. 2. Because it is done already in Latine by Dr. *Young* in his *Dies Dominica* (under the name of *Theophilus Loncardiensis* ;) which I take to be the moderatest, soundest and strongest Treatise on this subject that I have seen ; Though Mr. *Cawdry*, and *Palmer* (joyntly) have done well and at greater length: and Mr. *Eaton*, Mr. *Shephard*, Dr. *Bound*, *Wallæus*, *Rivet*, and my dear friend Mr. *George Abbot* against *Broad* have said very much: And in their way, Dr. *White*, Dr. *Heylin*, Bishop *Ironside*, Mr. *Brierwood*, &c. 3. I chose most of the same Citations which Dr. *Heylin* himself produceth, because he being the man that I am most put to defend my self against, his confessions are my advantage. 4. And if I had been willing, I could not have been so full in this, as the Subject will bespeak, because I have almost eleven years been separated from my Library, and long from the neighbourhood of any ones else.

I much pitty and wonder at those Godly men, who are so much for stretching the words of Scripture, to a sense that other men cannot find in them, as that in the word
[*Graven*

[*Graven Images*] in the second Commandment, they can find all set Formes of Prayer, all composed studyed Sermons, and all things about Worship of mans invention to be *Images* or Idolatry ; and yet they cannot find the abrogation of the Jewish Sabbath in the express words of *Col.* 2. 16: nor the other Texts which I have cited ; nor can they find the Institution of the Lords day in all the Texts and Evidences produced for it. But though Satan may somewhat disturbe our Concord and tempt some mens Charity to remissness, by these differences, he shall never keep them out of Heaven, who worship God, through Christ, by the Spirit, even in spirit and truth : Nor, shall he, I hope ever draw me, to think such holy persons as herein differ from me, to be worse than my self, though I think them in this to be

un-

The Preface.

unhappily mistaken: much less to approve either of their own *separation* from others, or of other mens condemning them as Hereticks, and inflicting severities upon them, for these their opinions sake.

THE

THE CONTENTS.

CHAP. I.

THE *state of the Question*, with the *summary proof of the Divine separation of the Lords Day,* page 1.

CHAP II.

That Christ commissioned his Apostles as his principal Church-Ministers, to teach the Churches all his Doctrine, and to deliver them all his Commands and Orders, and so to settle and guide the first Churches.
p. 5.

CHAP.

The Contents.

CHAP. III.

Christ promised his Spirit to his Apostles to enable them to do what he had commissioned them to do, by leading them into all truth, and bringing his words and deeds to their remembrance, and by guiding them as his Churches Guides.
p. 9.

CHAP. IV.

Christ performed all these Promises to his Apostles, and gave them his Spirit to enable them to all their commissioned work.
p. 11

CHAP. V.

The Apostles did actually separate and appoint the first day of the Week for Holy Worship, especially in Church Assemblies. Which is explained in several subordinate Propositions; And proved 1. By Scripture; 2. By unquestionable History; And the validity of this proof evinced; and the denyers of it proved to subvert the Churches certainty of greater matters.
p. 12

CHAP.

The Contents.

CHAP. VI.

This act of the Apostles appointing the Lords Day for holy Worship, was done by the especial inspiration and guidance of the Holy Ghost. p. 69

CHAP. VII.

Whether the seventh day Sabbath should be still kept by Christians, as of Divine obligation? Neg. proved. Where is shewed how far the fourth Commandment is abrogated (and all the Law of Moses.) p. 71

CHAP. VIII.

Of the Beginning of the Day. p. 91

CHAP. IX.

How the Lords Day should be kept. Of the length of the time, and the Objection about weariness. p. 93

CHAP.

CHAP. X.

How the Lords Day should not be spent; or what is unlawful on it; Of worldly business: Of recreations: of Idleness, &c.
p. 108

CHAP. XI.

What things should not be scrupled as unlawful on the Lords Day. p. 129

CHAP. XII.

Of what importance the due observing of the Lords Day is. Many great Reasons for it. p. 139

CHAP. XIII.

What other Church Festivals, or separated Dayes are lawful. p. 148

The

THE CONTENTS OF THE Appendix.

CHAP. I.

An Answer to certain Objections against the Lords Day, p.157

CHAP. II.

An Answer to more Arguments for the seventh day Sabbath, p.180

CHAP. III.

Whether the seventh day Sabbath be part of the Law of Nature; or only a Positive Law? p.202

CHAP.

The Contents.

CHAP. IV.

Whether every word in the Decalogue be of the Law of Nature? and of perpetual obligation? And whether all that was of the Law of Nature was in the Decalogue?
p. 214

CHAP. V.

Whether the truest Antiquity be for the seventh day Sabbath, as kept by the Churches of Christ?
p. 220

The Divine Appointment of the LORDS DAY, proved, as a separated Day for holy Worship, especially in the Church-Assemblies: And consequently the Cessation of the Seventh-day-Sabbath.

CHAP. I.

THOUGH the principal thing desired by the Enquirers is, That I would prove to them the Cessation of the Seventh-day Sabbath, yet because they cast off the Lords day, which I take to be a far greater error and sin, than the observation of both dayes; and because that when I have proved the Institution of the Lords Day, I shall the more easily take them off the other, by proving that there are not two weekly dayes set apart by God for holy Worship: Therefore I will begin with the first Question, *Whether the Lords day, or first day of the week, be separated by Gods Institution*

B *for*

for holy Worship, *especially in publick Church-conventions?* Aff.

And here for the right stating of the Question, let it be noted, 1. That it is not the *Name* of a *Sabbath* that we now meddle with, or stand upon. Let us agree in the *Thing*, and we shall easily bear a difference about the name. Grant that it is [*A day separated by Gods Institution for holy Assemblies and Worship*] and then call it a *Sabbath* or [*the Lords day*] as you please. Though for my self, I add That [*the Lords day*] is the name that the Holy Ghost hath set upon it, and the name which the first Churches principally used; and that they call it also sometimes by the name of the *Christian Sabbath*; but that is only Analogically, as it is resembled to the *Jewish Sabbath*; and as they used the names [*Sacrifice* and *Altar*] * at the same time, for the Christians Commemoration of Christs Sacrifice in the Sacrament of the Lords Supper, and for the Table, or as Dr. *Young* saith, *pag.* 23. As in Scripture, *Baptism* is called *Circumcision*. And that very rarely too.

* I speak only *de facto*, how the Antients used these words.

2. That the Question of the manner of observing the Lords day, and what exercises of Worship it must be spent in, and what Diversions are lawful or unlawful, as also when the day beginneth, are not to be here medled with in the beginning, but afterwards, when the Divine Institution of the Day it self is, first sufficiently proved. Which is done as followeth.

Arg.

Arg. *That day which was separated to holy Worship by the Holy Ghost, was separated to holy Worship by God the Father and the Son. But the first day of the Week was separated to holy Worship by the Holy Ghost: Therefore the first day of the Week was separated to holy Worship, by God the Father and the Son.*

The Minor only needeth proof among Christians.

That day which was separated to holy Worship by the Apostles, by the inspiration of the Holy Ghost, was separated to holy Worship by the Holy Ghost. But the first day of the Week was separated to holy Worship by the Apostles by the inspiration of the Holy Ghost. Therefore the first day of the Week was separated to holy Worship by the Holy Ghost.

The Minor which only needeth proof, is thus proved.

That day which was separated to holy Worship by the Apostles who had the Holy Ghost promised them by Christ, and given them, to lead them into all truth, and to bring all his Doctrines to their remembrance, and to teach the Churches to do all his Commands, and to feed, and guide, and order them, as his principal commissioned Church-Ministers, was separated to holy Worship by the Apostles by the inspiration of the Holy Ghost.

But such is the first day of the Week:

Therefore the first day of the Week is separated to holy Worship by the Apostles by the inspiration of the Holy Ghost.

I have five Propositions now distinctly to be proved: four for the proof of the Major, and

and one for the proof of the Minor.

The first Proposition is, *That Christ commissioned his Apostles as his principal Church-Ministers, to teach the Churches all his Doctrine, and deliver them all his Commands and Orders, and so to settle and guide the first Churches.*

The second Proposition is, *That Christ promised them his Spirit, to enable them to do what he had commissioned them to do, by leading them into all truth, and bringing his words and deeds to their remembrance, and by guiding them as his Churches Guides.*

The third Proposition is, *That Christ performed this promise, and gave his Spirit accordingly to his Apostles, to enable them to all their commissioned work.*

The fourth Proposition is, *That the Apostles did actually separate or appoint the first day of the Week, for holy Worship, especially in Church-assemblies.*

The fifth Proposition is, *That this act of theirs was done by the Guidance or inspiration of the Holy Ghost, which was given them.*

And when I have distinctly proved these five things, no sober understanding Christian can expect that I should prove any more, towards the proof of the Question in hand, Whether the first day of the Week be separated by Gods Institution for holy Worship, especially in Church-assemblies?

CHAP.

CHAP. II.

Prop. I. *That Christ Commissioned his Apostles, or his principal Church-Ministers, to teach the Churches all his Doctrine, and deliver them all his Commands and Orders, and so to settle and guide the first Churches.*

THis I prove, 1. By their Commission it self: 2. By their performance with its proper seal. 3. By the Consent of all the Christian world.

I. *Luke* 6. 13. *He called to him his Disciples, and of them he chose twelve, whom also he named Apostles.* Their first Commission is recited, *Matth.* 10. at large.

Matth. 28. 18, 19, 20. *All Authority is given me in Heaven and in Earth: Go ye therefore and disciple all Nations, baptizing them in the name of the Father, and of the Son, and of the Holy Ghost; Teaching them to observe all things whatsoever I have commanded you. And, loe, I am with you alway, even unto the end of the world; Amen.*

John 20. 21. *Then said Jesus to them again, Peace be unto you; As the Father hath sent me, even so send I you: And when he had said this, he breathed on them, and said, Receive ye the Holy Ghost: Whosesoever sins ye remit, they are remitted unto them, and whosesoever sins ye retain, they are retained.*

Luke 10. 16. Even of the seventy it is said, *He that heareth you, heareth me, and he that de-*
spiseth

(6)

spiseth you, despiseth me, and he that despiseth me, despiseth him that sent me. And to the twelve, Matth. 10. 40. *He that receiveth you, receiveth me,* &c.

Acts 26. 17. *Delivering thee from the people, and from the Gentiles, to whom now I send thee, to open their eyes.*

1 Cor. 15. 3. *For I delivered to you first of all that which I also received,* &c.

1 Cor. 11. 23. *For I received of the Lord, that which also I delivered unto you.*

1 Cor. 4. 1, 2. *Let a man so account of us as of the Ministers of Christ, and Stewards of the mysteries of God.*

Gal. 1. 11, 12. *But I certifie you, brethren, that the Gospel which was preached of me, is not after man; For I neither received it of man, neither was I taught it, but by the revelation of Jesus Christ.*

John 21. 15, 16, 17. Simon *Son of* Jonas *lovest thou me——Feed my Lambs.*

Matth. 16. 19. *I will give unto thee the Keyes of the Kingdom of Heaven: and whatsoever thou shalt bind on Earth, shall be bound in Heaven: and whatsoever thou shalt loose on Earth, shall be loosed in Heaven.*

John 17. 18. *As thou hast sent me into the world, so have I also sent them into the world.* See John 13. 16, 20.

Acts 1. 24, 25. *Shew whether of these two thou hast chosen, that he may take part of this Ministry and Apostleship, from which* Judas *by transgression fell.*

Gal. 1. 1. Paul *an Apostle, not of men, neither by man, but by Jesus Christ and God the Father.*

Acts 1. 2. *After that he through the Holy Ghost,*

Ghost, had given commandment to the Apostles whom he had chosen; to whom also he presented himself alive after his passion, by many infallible proofs, being seen of them forty dayes, and speaking of the things pertaining to the Kingdom of God.

Acts 2. 42. *They continued stedfast in the Apostles doctrine and fellowship*, &c.

Eph. 4. 11, 12, 13, 14, 15, 16. *He gave some Apostles, some Prophets*, &c.

1 Cor. 12. 28, 29. *First Apostles, secondarily Prophets*, &c. *Are all Apostles*, &c.

Eph. 2. 20. *Being built on the foundation of the Apostles*, &c.

2 Pet. 3. 2. *That ye may be mindfull of the words which were spoken before by the holy Prophets, and of the Commandments of us the Apostles of the Lord and Saviour.*

Acts 10. 5. *Send men to Joppa, and call for Simon*, &c. *and he shall tell thee*, &c.

They that will not take all this plain evidence of Scripture for a proof of this first Proposition, I suppose would not be ever the more moved by it, if I should be so needlesly tedious, as to stay to fetch Arguments from each Text.

2. The Apostles *exercised* such a power, as the Proposition mentioneth, and God set to it, the seal of Miracles. Therefore such a Power or Office was given them by Christ.

The Consequence is undenyable. The Antecedent of this *Enthimeme* is so plainly expressed in Scripture, that I am loth to take up much of my own or the Readers time, in proving so known a thing.

They founded the Churches; they delivered them the Doctrine and Commands of Christ; they setled the Churches, as to Officers, Orders, and Discipline, according to Christs Commands and the Spirits determinations: Thus they ordained the new Office of Deacons, and Deaconesses or Widows; and they ordained them Elders in every Church, or City; and they determined of Church Controversies; and gave the Church Decrees; and delivered the Will of Christ about the Sacrament, Church-Assemblies, Prophecyings, *&c. Acts* 2. *&* 14. 23. *Acts* 6. 3, 4, *&c.* 1 *Tim.* 3. *Titus* 1. *Acts* 15. 1 *Cor.* 11, 1 *Cor.* 14. *&c.*

3. That all Christians (save Hereticks) did acknowledge their power, and acquiesce in their Decrees and Conduct, being a matter of fact, needs no other proof, than the common History of former Ages; and practice of this. Which are so well known, that I will not injure the Reader by proving it.

CHAP.

CHAP. III.

Prop. 2. *Christ promised his Spirit to his Apostles, to enable them to do, what he had commissioned them to do, by leading them into all truth, and bringing his words and deeds to their remembrance, and by guiding them as his Churches Guides.*

IN the Old Testament it is prophesied and promised, Jer. 3. 15. *And I will give you Pastors according to mine heart, which shall feed you with knowledge and understanding.*

See all the Texts that promise the pouring out of the Spirit, *Isa.* 44. 3. *Ezek.* 36. 27. & 37. 14. & 39. 29. *Joel* 2. 28, 29. Which were principally fulfilled on the Apostles.

Luke 24. 49. *And behold, I send the promise of my Father upon you: But tarry ye in the City of Jerusalem, untill ye be endued with power from on high.*

John 15. 26, 27. *But, when the Advocate is come, whom I will send unto you from the Father, he shall testifie of me: and ye also shall bear witness, because ye have been with me from the beginning.*

John 16. 7, 12, 13, 14, 15. *It is expedient for you, that I go away; for if I go not away, the Advocate will not come unto you: But if I depart, I will send him unto you——I have yet many things to say unto you, but ye cannot bear them now. Howbeit when he, the Spirit of truth is come, he will*

will guide you into all the truth. For he shall not speak of himself; but whatsoever he shall hear, that shall he speak: And he shall shew you things to come. He shall glorifie me; for he shall receive of mine, and shew it unto you. All things that the Father hath are mine. Therefore said I that he shall take of mine, and shall shew it unto you.

John 17. 8. I have given to them the words which thou gavest me, and they have received them --- V. 17, 18. Sanctifie them through thy truth: thy word is truth: As thou hast sent me into the world, so have I also sent them into the world: And for their sakes I sanctifie my self, that they also might be sanctified through the truth.

Matth. 28. 20. Teaching them to observe all things whatsoever I have commanded you; and loe I am with you alwayes to the end of the world.

Acts 1. 4. And being assembled together with them, commanded them that they should not depart from Jerusalem, but wait for the promise of the Father which ye have heard of me. For John truly baptized with water; but ye shall be baptized with the Holy Ghost not many dayes hence. V. 8. But ye shall receive Power after that the Holy Ghost is come upon you, and ye shall be witnesses unto me, both in Jerusalem, and to all Judæa, and in Samaria, and unto the uttermost parts of the earth.

By these Texts it is most evident that Christ promiseth the Apostles an extraordinary Spirit, or measure of the Spirit, so to enable them to deliver his Commands, and execute their Commission, as that he will own what they do by the guidance thereof; and the Churches may rest upon it as the Infallible revelation of the Will of God.

CHAP.

Prop. 3. *Christ performed all these promises to his Apostles, and gave them his Spirit to enable them for all their commissioned work.*

THis is proved both from the fidelity of Christ, and from the express assertions of the Scripture. *He is faithful that hath promised.* Heb. 10. 23. Titus 1. 2. *God that cannot lye hath promised.* 2 Cor. 1. 18. *As God is true———* Rev. 6. 10. *How long O Lord, Holy and True———* Rev. 19. 11. *He was called faithful and true———* Rom. 3. 4. *Let God be true, and every man a lyar————* 1 John 5. 10 *He that believeth not God, hath made him a lyar.*

John 20. 22. *He breathed on them, and saith unto them, Receive ye the Holy Ghost.*

Acts 2. Containeth the Narrative of the comeing down of the Holy Ghost upon them, at large.

Acts 15. 28. *It seemed good to the Holy Ghost and to us———*

Heb. 2. 4. *God also bearing them witness, both with signs and wonders, and with divers mighty works, and distributions of the Holy Ghost according to his own will.*

1 Pet. 1. 12. *The things which are now reported unto you, by them that have preached the Gospel unto you, by the Holy Ghost sent down from Heaven———*

Rom.

Rom. 15. 19, 20. *Through mighty signs and wonders, by the power of the Spirit of God, so that from* Jerusalem, *and round about to Illyricum I have fully preached the Gospel of Christ.*

Read all the Texts in *Acts* and elsewhere, that speak of all the Apostles Miracles, and their giving of the Holy Ghost, *&c.* And 1 *Cor.* 7. 40. *Acts* 4. 8, 31. *Acts* 5. 3. *&* 6. 3. *&* 7. 51, 55. *&* 8. 15, 17, 18, 19. *&* 9. 17. *&* 10. 44, 45, 47. *&* 11. 15, 16, 24. *&* 13. 2, 4, 9, 52. *&* 16. 6. *Rom.* 5. 5. *&* 9. 1. 1 *Cor.* 2. 13. 2 *Tim.* 1. 14. 1 *Cor.* 12. *Eph.* 4. 7, 8, *&c.* *&* 3. 5. But this Proposition is confessed by all Christians.

CHAP. V.

Prop. 4. *The Apostles did actually separate and appoint the first day of the Week for holy Worship, especially in Church-Assemblies.*

HEre the Reader must remember, that it is *meer matter of fact*, that is to be proved in the proof of this Proposition; and that *all till this*, is clearly and undenyably proved; so that the whole Controversie resteth upon the proof of the *fact!* That indeed *The Apostles did separate or set apart this day for ordinary* (publick) *Worship.*

And in order to the fuller proof of this, I have these subordinate Propositions to prove.

Prop.

Prop. 1. *Matter of past fact is to be known to us by History* (Written, Verbal or Practical.)

This is evident in the nature of the thing. *History* is the Narration of *facts* that are past. We speak not of the fact of meer *natural agents*, but of *Moral* or *humane* facts. It may be known without History what *Eclipses* there have been of the *Sun*; what changes of the Moon, &c. But not what in particular *Morals* have been done by man.

The necessity of *other distinct* wayes of knowledge, are easily disproved. 1. It need not be known by *Divine supernatural Revelation*. Otherwise no men could know what is past, but *Prophets* or inspired persons: nor Prophets but in few things: For it cannot be proved, that God ever revealed to Prophets or inspired persons, the general knowledge of things past; but only some *particulars* of special use (as the *Creation* to *Moses, &c.*) so that if Revelation by *Inspiration*, Voice or Visions, were necessary, Scripture it self could be understood by none but inspired persons, or that had such revelation.

2. It is not known by *Natural Causes*, and by arguing from the Natural Cause to the Effects. It is no more possible to know all things *past* this way, (by knowing the Causes) than all things *future*. Therefore it must be ordinarily known by *Humane report*, which we call *History* or *Tradition*.

Prop. 2. *Scripture History is not the only certain History*; *much less the only credible*.

Without Scripture History we may be certain, that there was in 1666. a great Fire in *London*,

don, and a great plague in 1665. and that there were Wars in *England*, 1642, 1643, *&c.* and that there have been Parliaments in *England* which have made the Statutes now in force; and that there have been such Kings of *England* for many Ages, as our Records and Histories mention, *&c.*

Prop. 3. *Scripture History is not the only certain History of the things of the Ages in which it was written, or of former Ages; much less the only credible History of them.*

We may know by other History certainly, that there were such persons as *Cyrus, Alexander, &c.* That the *Macedonians*, had a large extended Empire; that the *Romans* after by many Victories obtained a spacious Empire; that there were such persons as *Julius Cæsar, Augustus, Tiberius, Nero, Cicero, Virgil, Horace, Ovid,* &c.

Prop. 4. *Scripture History is not the only means appointed by God, to help us to the knowledge of Ecclesiastical matters of fact, transacted in Scripture times.*

1. For if *Humane History* be *certain* or *credible* in *other cases*, it is *certain* or *credible* in *these*. There being no reason why *these* things, or *much* of them, should not be as capable of a certain delivery to us by humane History as other matters. As that there were Christians in those times, may be known by what *Tacitus, Suetonius, &c.* say. And the antient Writers oft appeal in many cases to the Heathens own History. And no man pretendeth as to the Civil matters mentioned in the Scriptures, that no other History of the same is credible or certain. As of the Government

vernment of *Augustus, Tiberius, Herod, Pilate, Fœlix, Festus,* &c.

2. There are other certain means known to us; of which I must refer the Reader to what I have written in my Reasons of the Christian Religion, *Part* 2. *Cap.* 7. specially *pag.* 335. to 340.

3. No man can doubt but that the Christians of that same age, (as till the year one hundred) might easily and certainly know such a matter of publick fact, as whether the *Lords day* was constantly set apart and observed by all the Christian Churches for holy Worship: For 1. It is certain that they did know it by *sight and sense*, and therefore had no need of *History*. 2. It is certain that they knew it *before the Scriptures were written*, which we now speak of: For it is not possible that for all those years time before any of the New Testament was written, the Christians who assembled to worship God, should not know on what day they used to assemble.

And if they knew it in the year 100. they must needs know it as well in the year 101. & 102. & 103. and so on. For those that were young Christians fifty years after Christ, would be aged at an hundred: And those that were young at an hundred, would be aged at an hundred and fifty, and so on. So that an age of people, not ending at the age of a single person, Congregations and societies are like Rivers, that keep the same channel, and name, while one part of water followeth another. Nay, some of the *same men* are there *anno* 100. who were there *anno* 50. some *anno* 150. who were there *anno* 100. and

so

so on. Ten thousand thousand men, women and children, can tell on what day the Congregations of *England* use to assemble; whereas if an *Apostle* were among us, and should *write* on what day we assemble; fewer would know it by that means; And they that knew it but by his *writing*, would know it *less confidently*, than they that knew it by *sense* and *experience*.

Yet, forget not, that I am far from ascribing a certainty or a credibility to *all* humane History: Much more from equalling any with the credit of Divine History. But only I say, 1. That *sense* is more assuring, as to the *subject*, than any History whatever: 2. And that some History besides Divine is certain: 3. And that much History is credible: 4. And that this instance of the Day on which all Churches in the world assembled for holy Worship, is one of the most palpable for certainty that possibly could be imagined.

4. And I add, that if *some* humane History or Tradition be not certain, there can be no certainty of much of the *Divine History*, to any but the persons who were themselves *inspired*, or that *saw the Visions*, or *Miracles* that confirmed them. For as *internal sense* or *intuition* must assure the *Inspired* persons themselves, and *external sense* must assure those that *saw the matters of fact*; so all the rest have no way to know them, but either still by a succession of *New Revelations* from Heaven, (which God doth not give) or else by *Report*. And I can no otherwise know what was revealed to an Apostle, nor what was done in those times: (Of which more anon.)

Prop.

Prop. 5. *The first institution of Church Offices, and Orders, and so of the Lords day, was not by Scripture.*

The proof is undeniable: Because the *Old Testament* did not contain the Institution, (e. g. of *particular Churches, Sacraments, Presbyters, Deacons, Deaconesses, and the Lords day,* &c.) And the *New Testament* was none of it written till *anno* 40. at soonest when some (as *Bucholtzer, Bellarm,*&c.) think *Matthews* Gospel was written, though others say many years after,) and it was not *all written* till *ann.* 99. Now it is certain that the Church was not all these years without the *Orders* now in question, nor without *a day* to meet on for publick Worship. Even as *Baptism* and the *Lords Supper* were instituted by Christ himself, long before the writing of any part of the New Testament, and the Church was in long possession of them, upon the bare verbal declaration of the Apostles.

Prop. 6. *Therefore it is certain that no part of the New Testament was written to any such end as to institute Sacraments, or Church Offices, or standing Orders; but to instruct men about those that were already instituted,* (as to the use of *those times.*)

For it could not be written to institute that which was instituted before, so many years.

Prop. 7. *No part of the New Testament was written to make known to the Churches of those times, the said Sacraments, Offices, stated Orders, and Time of Worship;* (Still observe that by a *part* I mean any *book*; And I except the *Decree*, written in a Letter of the Apostles, Elders and Brethren,

Brethren, *Act.* 15. concerning Circumcision, not to be imposed on the Gentiles; which yet made no new institution, nor declared any, but only determined of the continued forbearance of some things forbidden before of God, in the precepts called *Noah*'s; and *Pauls* Epistles, which reduce the Churches to Orders before setled, and urge them to duty, and decide some doubts about particular cases of Conscience.)

The proof is visible, 1. In the Writings themselves: 2. In that all the Churches were in the possession and use of all the things in question, long before: (For *mutable Orders* and *Circumstances* are none of the things in question.) It would be vain to write a history now, to tell English men of this present age, that the Lords day is used in *England* as a day set apart for publike worship; or that persons are Baptized, or receive the Lords Supper in *England*. For seeing it is the common usage of all the Christians almost of the Land, it is needless to tell men among us by writing that it is so (unless it be to inferr somewhat else from it.)

Prop. 8. *Yet those holy Scriptures which were written to men of those times, were also intended for the instruction of all succeeding ages; And so the foure Evangelists wrote the history of Christ,* and Luke *wrote the history of* Paul *till his coming to* Rome *and longer, and of some more of the Apostles; And on the by, in the Epistles extant, the Churches Customes of those times are much intimated; And all this together with the subordinate history and the universal tenure and practice of the Churches, is that history by which we must know*

the

the matters of fact of those times; Nor is there any room left for a rational pretense of *Rome* or any other Church, to produce Divine Institutions, which were committed *only to them*, or entrusted to *their particular keeping* only; and were not delivered in *Scripture*, not in *Common* to the *whole Church*.

Prop. 9. *Thus according to the use of the writings of the New Testament, the matter of fact in question* (of the *Lords dayes separation*) *is historically touched on, and proved; though but briefly and on the by, as a thing as well known to the Church before, as what day goeth over their head.*

The Historical hints of the New Testament must be taken together, and not a part only; that they may prove a usage.

And, 1. That *Christ rose* on that day is past doubt among Christians. *Joh.* 20. 1. *Luk.* 24. 1. *Mar.* 16. 2. *Matth.* 28. 1.

2. On that same day he taught the two disciples, *Luk.* 24. 13. And the same day he appeared to the Disciples, and instructed them, and did eate with them, *Luk.* 24. 33, 36. There the Disciples were assembled, and there he blessed them, gave them their Commission, and the Holy Ghost, *Joh.* 20. 19, 20, 21, 22.

3. The next first day of the week Christ chose to appear to them again, when *Thomas* was with them, and convinced him, *Joh.* 20. 26.

4. In *Act.* 20. 7. It is mentioned as the day of their *Assembling to break bread* (which though they did oft on other daies, yet no day else was *peculiarly appointed* for it,) As for the dissenters cavil about the Translation of Ἐν τῇ μιᾷ τῶν σαββάτων,

βάτων, Beza hath given them Reason enough against it; And *Grotius* and almost all expositors are against them: And most that translate it literally *una Sabbatorum*, take *Una* and *Prima* here to be all one. And *Calvin* with others noteth, that the same phrase being used of the day of the Resurrection, *Matth.* 26. 1. *Luk.* 24. 1. *Joh.* 20. 1. will direct us to expound this; unless you mean also to deny the Resurrection to have been on the *first day*.

And 1 *Cor.* 16. 1, 2. χτ μίαν must needs have the same signification; And *Mark* 26. 9. compared with the other Evangelists so expounds them as *Beza* noteth; who also telleth us *that in one old Copy* he found added [*the Lords day*] and citeth *Hierome adv. Vigilant.* saying [*Per unam Sabbati ; hoc est, in die Dominico,* &c.] And Dr. *Hammond* well noteth that it plainly relateth to the Christian assemblies, to which they were not to come empty, but to deposite what they brought into the treasury of the Church; or if it were in their *private repositories*, it doth not much difference the case. *Calvins* exception against *Chrysostome* here is groundless, as the reasons before evince. So that by this Text the custome of holding Church meetings on the Lords day, as a peculiar day, is intimated, though but on the by, as most Expositors agree.

And the denomination of the *Lords day*, Joh. 1. 10. being the same which the Christian Churches ever used of the First day, puts it yet further out of doubt. As for his conjecture who doubteth whether it may be meant of the Anniversary

versary day of Christs Resurrection, when as the constant use of the name by all the Churches, sheweth that it was taken ever since for the *weekly* day, it deserveth no other refutation.

Now though all this set together shew that Scripture is not silent of the matter of fact; yet it is the full and unquestionable expository evidence of the practice of all Churches in the world, since the very daies of the Apostles, which beyond all doubt assureth us that *de facto* the Lords day was by the Apostles separated for holy Worship, especially in publick Church-assemblies. But these several intimations being seconded with so full an Exposition, tell us that the Scripture is not silent in the case, nor doth pass it by. I was loth to name the day of the sending down of the Holy Ghost as a proof : Because that some do controvert it. But it seemeth to me a very considerable thing. 1. That the day (that year) of the conclusion of Pentecost on which the Holy Ghost was given, was indeed the first day of the week, even Dr. *Heylin* granteth without any question or stop. And the Churches observation of *Whitsunday* as the day, and that so very early as *Epiphanius* and many others say, from the Apostles, doth seem a very credible history or tradition of it. 2. Its agreed on that the Passover that year fell on the Sabboth day, and that Pentecost was fifty daies after the Passover: which falleth out on the Lords day. And *Grotius* noteth from *Exod*. 19. 1. that it was the day that the Law was given on, and so on which the Spirit was given for the new Law. 3. And considering that this great gift of the Holy Ghost which

which was to make the Apostles Infallible, and to enable them for their commission-work, and bring all Chrifts Doctrines and Commands to their remembrance, was so memorable a thing, that it was as it were the *Beginning* of the *full Gospel-state* of the *Church*, and *Kingdom* of Chrift, (which through all Chrifts abode on Earth, was as the *Infant, existent* indeed but in the *womb*, and on this day was as it were *Born* before the world, and brought into the open light;) the *Lords day* also seemeth to me to be as it were *Conceived* on the *day of Chrifts Resurrection*, but *Born* on this day of the Holy Ghofts descent.

But Dr. *Heylin* hath one poor reason againft it, viz. *Because it was but an accidental thing that the day fell out that year on the first day.*

Answ. 1. Was it not according to the course of Nature? How then can that be called Accidental? 2. But however it was no contingent accidental thing (in his sense) that the *Holy Ghoft was sent down on that day* rather than another. If a sparrow fall not to the ground without Gods providence, did God choose that day He knew not why? Or did it fall out hap hazard or by chance?

I need not insist on the confutation of his Cavils about the other Texts forecited. Note only, 1. That as to his exception about Chrifts travel on his Resurrection day, I have after answered it. 2. That he freely granteth that μιᾷ τῶν σαββάτων, signifieth *The first day* of the week, both in *Act.* 20. 7. and 1 *Cor.* 16. 2. 3. That he himself citeth afterward many teftimonies that oblations and contributions were in the Churches a ufual

Lords

Lords dayes work. 4. That he confesseth that *Rev.* 10. 1. is meant of the Lords day, as by that time grown into reputation. 5. That he thinketh it was in small reputation before, because *Paul* chose the Sabbath so often to Preach on, to the Jews and Hellenists, or Greeks: whereas he himself is forced to confess that it was not for the *dayes* sake, but the *Assemblies,* to do them good. 6. That he vainly conceiteth [that Because the Lords day was kept on the account of *Chrifts Refurrection,*] it implyeth that it was not kept by *Gods command*; which needeth no confutation. 7. That his labour to prove that *Paul* meant the Jewish Sabbath as abrogated is vain; for we deny it not. 8. That he cannot deny that Christians had all that time of the Apostles a *stated day* (as *Pliny* himself witnesseth) for solemn worship, above other daies. 9. That he vainly snatcheth a little countenance from *Calvin* and *Beza,* &c. when as no man since *Cochlæus* writeth more detestably of them. 10. That after he confesseth that [*its no doubt* but the *Religious observation of the day began in the Apostles age with their approbation* and Authority, *and hath since continued in the same respect.*] And what needs he more for confutation?

And as to his allegations of the Judgement of the Reformed, Lutheran and Roman Church, 1. We take none of them for our Rule (so impartial are we) But, 2. He himself citeth *Beza, Mercer, Paræus, Cuchlinus, Simler, Hospinian, Zanchius, &c.* as holding that *It was, an*

C 4 *Apostolical*

Apostolical and *Truly Divine Tradition, that the Apostles turned the Sabbath into the Lords day, that it was an Apostolical custome, or a custome received in the Apostles times,* &c.

And whereas afterward he would perswade us that they spent but a little of the day in holy worship, he himself cited Mr. *George Sandys* Travels, saying of the Copties, that [*On Saturday presently after midnight, they repair unto their Churches, where they remain well nigh till Sunday at noon* (of the Evening he speaketh not, but of their first meeting) *during which time they neither sit nor kneel, but support themselves on Crutches; And they sing over the most part of* Davids *Psalms at every meeting with divers parcels of the New Testament*] (This is like the old way; And such a Liturgie we do not contradict nor scruple.)

Sandys also informeth us of the *Armenian* Christians that *coming into the place of the Assembly on* Sunday *in the afternoon* (no doubt they had been there in the Morning) *he found one sitting in the midst of the Congregation, in habit not differing from the rest, reading on a Bible in the Chaldean tongue: That anon after, came the Bishop in a hood or Vest of black, with a staffe in his hand? That first he prayed, and then sung certain Psalms assisted by two or three. After all of them singing joyntly, at interims praying to themselves, the Bishop all this while with his hands erected and his face towards the Altar; That Service being ended, they all kissed his hand, and bestowed their Almes, he laying his other hand on their heads, and blessing them,* &c.

And

And of the Abassines he reciteth out of *Brierwood*, (and he from *Damianus* a *Goes*) that they honour the Lords day as the *Christian Sabbath*, and the *Saturday* as the Jews Sabbath, because they receive the Canons called the Apostles which speak for both.

And King *Edgar* in *England* ordained that the Sabbath should begin on *Saturday* at three a Clock Afternoon, and continue till break a Day on *Munday*. These Laws for the Sabbath of *Alfred*, *Edgar*, &c. were confirmed by *Etheldred*, and more fully by *Canutus*.

But of these things I shall say more anon under the Proposition following ; In the mean time only remembring you, 1. That it is well that we are required after the fourth Commandment to pray [*Lord have Mercy upon us, and encline our hearts to keep this Law*] And we accept his Concession, that this includeth all of that Commandment which is the Law of Nature (Though I have told you that it reacheth somewhat further.) 2. That we approve of the plain Doctrine of the English Homilies on this point, and stand to the Exposition of sober impartiality.

Prop. 10. *It hath been the constant practice of all Christs Churches in the whole world, ever since the daies of the Apostles to this day, to assemble for publick worship on the Lords day, as a day set apart thereunto by the Apostles. Yea so universal was this judgement and practice, that there is no one Church, no one writer, or one heretick* (that I remember to have read of) *that can be proved ever to have dissented or gainsaid it, till of late times.*

The

The proof of this is needless to any one that is versed in the writings of the ancients; And others cannot try what we shall produce. I have been these ten years separated from my Library, and am therefore less furnished for this task than is requisite: But I will desire no man to receive more, than the Testimonies produced by Dr. *Pet. Heylin* himself, which with pittiful weakness he would pervert. And he being the Grand Adversary with whom I do now contend, I shall only premise these few Observations, as sufficient to confute all his Cavils and Evasions.

1. When his great work is to prove that the Lords day was not called the *Sabbath* (unless by allusion) we grant it him (as to a Jewish Sabbath) as nothing to the purpose.

2. Whereas he strenuously proveth that the Lords day was not taken for a *Sabbath de re*, we grant it him also, taking the word in the primitive Jewish sense.

3. When he laboureth to prove that Christians met on other daies of the week besides the Lords day (though not for the Lords Supper) we grant it him as nothing to the purpose. So *Calvin* Preached or Lectured daily at *Geneva*, and yet kept not every day as a holy day separated to Gods worship, as they did the Lords day, though too remisly. So we do still keep Weekday Lectures, and the Church of *England* requireth the Reading of Common Prayer on *Wednesdayes* and *Fridays*, and holy day Evens; Do they therefore keep them Holy as the Lords day?

4. When

4. When he tells us that *Clemens Alexandrinus* and *Origen*, plead against them that would hear and pray on that day only, we grant it him; and we are ready to say as they do, that we should not confine Gods Service to one day only, as if we might be profane and worldly on all other daies; but should take all fit opportunities for religious helps, and should all the week keep our minds as near as we can in a holy frame and temper. Of the rest of his Objections I shall say more in due place.

5. But I must note in the beginning that he granteth the main cause which I plead for, acknowledging, *Hist. Sab. l. 2. page 30.* it thus; [" *So that the Religious observation of this day,* " *beginning in the age of the Apostles, no doubt but* " *with their Approbation and Authority, and since* " *continuing in the same respect for so many* " *ages, may be very well accounted amongst* " *those Apostolical Traditions, which have been* " *universally received in the Church of God.*] And what need we more than the *Religious* Observation, *in the Apostles time,* by the *Apostles Approbation* and *Authority, and this delivered to us by the universal Church,* as an *Apostolical Tradition.*

But yet he saith that the Apostles made it not a *Sabbath*. *Answ.* Give us the *Religious observation,* and call it by what name you please. We are not fond of the name of the Sabbath.

6. And therefore we grant all that he laboriously proveth of the abolition of the Jewish Sabbath, and that the Ancients commonly consent, that by the abolished Sabbath, *Col.* 2. 16. is

meant

meant inclusively the weekly Jewish Sabbath: *Epiphan. l.* 1. *hæref.* 33. *n.* 11. *Ambrof. in loc. Hieron. Epist. ad Alguf.* qu.10.*Chrysost.Hom.*13. *in Hebr.* 7. *August. cont. Jud.* cap. 2. *& cont. Fauft. Manich. l.* 16. *c.* 28. I recite the places for them that doubt of it.

Now let us peruse the particular Testimonies.

1. I begin with *Ignatius,* (though *Dallæus* have said so much to prove the best Copy of him of latter date and spurious; because others think otherwise, and that Copy is by him thought to be written *Cent.* 3.) who saith [*Let us not keep the Sabbath in a Jewish manner in sloth and idleness, but after a spiritual manner; not in bodily ease, but in the study of the Law; not eating meat drest yesterday, or drinking warm drinks, and walking out a limited space, but in the contemplation of the works of God———And after the Sabbath let every one that loveth Christ keep the Lords day Festival, the Resurrection day, the Queen and Empress of all daies, in which our life was raised again, and death was overcome by our Lord and Saviour.*]

Either these *Epist.* of *Ignatius* (*ad Philip. &c.*) are genuine or spurious. If genuine, then note how clearly it is asserted that the Lords day was to be observed as the Queen of all daies, by all that were lovers of Christ. And that the seventh day Sabbath was kept with it then and there (in *Asia* so near the Apostles daies) no wonder; when it was but the honourable, gradual, receding from the Mosaical Ceremonies, with an avoiding the scandalous hinderance of the Jews Conversion. And Dr. *Heylin* well noteth, that it was

only

only the Eastern Churches next the Jews that for a time kept both daies, but not the Western, who rather turned the Sabbath to a fast.

But if *Ignatius Ep.* be spurious written *Cent.* 3. then as *Dallæus* would prove, they were written by some heretical or heterodox person; And so it will be no wonder that holy dayes are pleaded for, when (as Dr. *Heylin* observeth) *Cerinthus* and his followers in the Apostles times, stood up for the Jewish Sabbath and Ceremonies, and so were for both daies: But it will be our Confirmation that even the Hereticks held with the universal Church for the Lords day.

2. The great Controversie about the Day of *Easter*, which spread so early through all the Churches is a full Confirmation of our matter of *fact*. For when the Western Churches were for the *Passover day* (the better to content the Jews saith *Heylin*) the Eastern thought it intollerable that it should not be kept on a *Lords* day, because that was the weekly day observed on the same account of the Resurrection: The Eastern Churches never questioned their supposition of the *Lords day*; And the Western (after *Victors* rash excommunicating the *Asian* Bishops) never rested till they brought them to keep it on the Lords day: *Pius, Anicetus, Victor*, &c. prosecuting the cause.

3. The Book (though perished) which *Melito* wrote *of the Lords day*, *Euseb. l.* 4. *c.* 25. by the title may be well supposed to confirm at least the matter of fact or usage.

4. All those little Councils, mentioned by *Heylin, p.* 48. held at *Osroena, Corinth*, in *Gaul*,
in

in *Pontus*, in *Rome* prove this, *The Canons of them all,* saith *Heylin, being extant in* Eusebius's *time, and in all which it was concluded for the Sunday.*

But saith *Heylin* by this [*You see that the Sunday and the Sabbath were long in striving for the Victory*] *p.* 49. *Answ.* I see that some men can out-face the clearest light. Here was no striving at all which day should be the weekly day set apart for holy worship; but only whether *Easter* should follow the time of *Pentecost*, or be confined to the Lords day.

5. *Justin Martyrs* Testimony is so express and so commonly cited, that I need not recite the words at large [*Upon the Sunday all of us assemble in the Congregation———Upon the day called Sunday all within he Cities or in the Countrey, do meet together in some place, where*, &c.] He proceedeth to shew the worship there performed.

Now 1. Here being mention of no other day, no man can question but that this day was set apart for these holy assemblies in a peculiar manner as the other week dayes were not. 2. This being the writing of one of the most Learned and antient of all the Christian Writers. 3. And being purposely written to one of the wisest of all the Emperours, as an Apologie for all the Christians: 4. And being written at *Rome*, where the matter of fact was easily known, deserveth as much credit as any Christian History or Writing since the Apostles can deserve. Nor hath *Heylin* any thing to say against it.

6. The next remembred by *Heylin* is *Dionysius Corinth.* who lived 175. cited out of *Eusebius Hist.*

Hist. l. 4. c. 22. [*To day we keep the Holy Lords day, wherein we read the Epistle you wrote to us, &c.*] Against this *Heylin* saith not a word.

7. The next is *Clemens Alexandr.* who expresly asserteth the matter of fact, that the Lords day was then kept by Christians. Yea, *Heylin* derideth him for fetching it as far as *Plato Strom. l. 7.* But *Heylin* thinks he was against keeping any dayes: But he that will examine his words shall find, that he speaketh only against them that would be Ceremonious observers of the day, more than of the work of the day, and would be religious on that day alone. And therefore he saith, that [*He that leadeth his life according to the Ordinances of the Gospel doth keep the Lords Day, when he casteth away every evil thought, and doing things with knowledge and understanding, doth glorifie the Lord in his Resurrection.*] This is not to speak against the Day, but to shew how it ought to be sincerely kept. But if he had been against it, its all one to my cause, who only prove that *de facto all Christian Churches kept it.*

8. The next witness is *Tertullian*, who oft asserteth this to be the holy day of the Christians Church-Assemblies, and holy Worship: His testimony in *Apolog. cap.* 16. is so commonly known that I need not recite it. It is the same in sense with *Justin Martyrs*, and written in an Apology for the Christians, purposely describing their custom of meeting and worshipping on the *Sunday* (as he calls it there) as *Justin* did. And that it was not an hours work only, he shews in saying, that *The day was kept as a day of rejoicing,*
and

and then describeth the work. And *de Idolol. c.* 14. he saith, that *every eighth day* was the Christians festival. And *de Coron. Mil. c.* 3. and oft he calleth it the Lords day, and saith it was a crime to fast upon it. And the work of the day described by *Justin*, and by him *Apolog. c.* 39. is just the same that we desire now the day to be spent in: we plead for no other.

But most grosly saith *Heylin*, pag. 55. [*But sure it is that their assemblies held no longer than our Morning Service; that they met only before noon; for* Justin *saith, that when they met they used to receive the Sacrament, and that the service being done, every man went again to his daily labours.*] *Answ.* Is this a proof to conclude a [*Certainty*] from? Most certainly abundance of testimonies might be produced to prove that they came together early in the Morning, and stayed till Evening, if not till within Night. The former *Pliny* and many others witness: And the later many accusations of the Heathens, that censured them for night-crimes at their meetings: And all that report it almost, tell us of the Sacrament administred, and *Tertullian* and others, of their feasting together (their Love Feasts) as a *Supper* before they parted: Now let but the time be measured by the work: By that time the Scriptures of the Old Testament and New were read, and all the prayers then made, and all the Preaching and Exhortations, and then all the Prayers and Praises at the Celebration of the Lords Supper (especially if they were half as long as the Liturgies ascribed to *Basil*, *Chrysostom*, and the rest in the *Biblioth. Patrum*) and by that

(33)

Sacrament it self was administred,
action and singing of Psalms, and
ions and Collections made ; and be-
ll the Church Discipline on parti-
s exercised, where Questions and
Proofs must take up a great deal
e one day would be at an end, or
And after when the Love Feasts
, and the Church met twice, and
ermission, they did as we do now.
Custom of Preaching all the Morn-
Audientes and *Catechumens*, till al-
when they were dismiss with a *Mis-*
spending the rest of the day in
e Church, and Celebrating the Sa-
h all the larger Eucharistical acts,
how the day was spent: Which
kly prove by particular Testimonies,
n separated from my Library; and
th fully done it to my hand. The
t of these testimonies, with what
hath of their Catechizing and
er will soon satisfie the impartial

he saith out of *Justin*, of *returning to*
I can find no such word in him; nor
here is any such to be found, unless
to their six dayes weekly labour,
eligious work was ended with the
imagine the Reader will find no
much.
t proof is universal, even the con-
ne Christian Churches without one
; Vote that ever I read of, that the
D   Lords

Lords dayes worship was to be performed *standing*, and that it was not allowed them to pray or worship kneeling, upon any Lords day in the year (or any week day between *Easter* and *Whitsontide*): And the difficulty of these stations is expressed (see *Albaspinæus* of it) which sheweth that it was for a long time. Whatever they did in Hearing (its like they sate, for *Justin* saith, We rise to pray) but it is certain they stood in *worshipping acts*, as *prayer* and *praise*. This *Justin Martyr* hath before mentioned: *Tertullian* hath it expresly, and *Heylin* himself citeth him *de Coron. Mil. & Basil l. de Spir. S. c.* 27. *& Hieron. advers. Luciferian. August. Epist.* 118. *Hilar. Præf. in Psal. Ambros. Serm.* 62. To which he may add *Epiphanius*, and divers Councils, especially *Nic.* 1. *& Trul.* of which after. (I once pleaded this ancient custom with them that would have all excluded from the Sacrament that kneel not, to prove that kneeling at the Sacrament on the Lords dayes could not be in the Church of many hundred years after the Apostles, when the universal Church condemned kneeling on all Lords dayes worship) And Dr. *Heylin* himself saith [*What time this custom was laid by I can hardly say; but sure I am, it was not laid aside in a long time after; not till the time of Pope* Alexander *the third, who lived about the year* 1160. *&c.*] Now from all this it is most evident that the Lords day was then observed.

10. In this place though by anticipation I add the two General Councils now named: The first great General Council at *Nice, Car.* 20. which

reneweth and confirmeth this antient custom of not kneeling in prayer on the Lords dayes, that there might be an uniformity kept in the Churches. And the *Concil. Contr. Trul.* have the same again; which proveth what we seek, the matter of fact of the dayes general observation.

11. The next is *Origen*, who is not denyed to witness to the matter of fact; but *Heylin* thinks he was against the *Right* of it: But his mistake is the same, as about *Clemens Alex*. *Origen* did but desire that other dayes might be kept also as profitably as they could; as our Lecture dayes are.

12. *Cyprian* is the next, whose testimonies for matter of fact are full, and *Heylin* hath nothing to say against him, but that it is his private opinion, that the Lords day was prefigured in the eighth day destined to Circumcision. Which is nothing at all to our business in hand.

13. And he himself cites Pope *Fabians* Decretal *Anno* 237. (a testimony therefore that he is not to refuse) [*for every man and woman on the Lords dayes to bring a quantity of bread and wine to be first offered on the Altar, and then distributed in the Sacrament*]

The Canon of *Clem.* before mentioned I now pretermit.

But saith Dr. *Heylin* 1. *All dayes between* Easter *and* Whitsunday *had adoration by genuflection also prohibited on them.* 2. *And the Church had other Festivals also.*

Answ. 1. The Reason of Station was to signifie Christs Resurrection and ours: Therefore it continued for these dayes: But that was for the short occasional meetings of those dayes, which he himself will not say were separated to worship. 2. And the other Festivals of the Church make nothing against us: For 1. Some of them (as *Easter* and *Whitsunday*) were but the same Lords day. 2. And some of them were but Anniversary, and not weekly Holy dayes; as the Nativity, &c. 3. And he confesseth even these were brought in long after the Apostles dayes, and therefore can lay no claim to Apostolical institution. Pag. 62. he himself saith, that [*The Feast of Christs Nativity was ordained or instituted in the second Century, and that of his Incarnation in the third.*] And besides *Easter* and *Whitsunday* (which are the Lords day) *Christmas* is all that he nameth out of *Beda* (so long after) as the *Majora Solennia*. The Eves were but hours for preparation.

14. To these (though in the fourth Century) I may add *Epiphanius*, who recordeth the Station (and Adoration to the East) on the Lords dayes as those Traditions received by the Universal Church.

And here I would have it specially noted, that when *Tertullian*, *Epiphanius* and others note *standing on the Lords dayes to be an unwritten Tradition received by the whole Church*, they do not say the same of the *Lords day it self*, (though the Antients oft say, that we *received it from the Apostles* :) Now by this it is plain, that they took the Lords day to be of Apostolick Institution past all question, and the unwritten *Universal Traditions* to be somewhat lower (which there was no Scripture for at all.) (Among which the

white

white Garment, and the Milk and Honey to the Baptized, and the Adoration toward the East are numbred.) For he that is appointed to worship on the Lords dayes *standing*, or toward the *East*, is supposed to know that on that day he is to worship. If the Mode on that *day* be of Universal Tradition as a Ceremony, the day is supposed to be somewhat more than of unwritten Tradition.

15. I add here also (though in the fourth Century, because it looks back to the Institution) the words of *Athanasius* cited by *Heylin* himself, *Homil. de Semente* (though *Nannius* question it) [*That our Lord transferred the Sabbath to the Lords day.*] But saith Dr. Heylin [*This must be understood, not as if done by his Commandment, but on his occasion: the Resurrection of our Lord on that day, being the principal Motive which did influence his Church to make choice thereof for the Assemblies——For otherwise it would cross what formerly had been said by* Athanasius *in his* τιμᾶμεν, *&c.*]. *Answ.* It expresseth the common judgement of the Church, that Christ himself made the Change by these degrees: 1. Fundamentally and as an Exemplar by his own Resurrection on that day; giving the first cause of it, as the Creation-rest did of the seventh day: 2. Secretly commanding it to his Apostles. 3. Commissioning them to promulgate all his Commands. 4. Sending down the Spirit on that very day. 5. And by that Spirit determining them by promulgation to determine publickly of the day, and settle all the Churches in long possession of it before their death. That which

is thus done, may well be said to be done by Christ, 2. And what shew of Contradiction hath his Τιμᾶμῳ to this? [*It was commanded at first that the Sabbath day should be observed in memory of the accomplishment of the World: so do we celebrate the Lords day as a Memorial of the beginning of a new Creation.*] Had not he a Creating head here that out of these words could gather, that we celebrate the Lords day *without a command Voluntarily?* One would think [*so*] should signifie the contrary.

But *ib. pag.* 8. he citeth *Socrates* for the same, saying that [*The designe of the Apostles was not to busie themselves in prescribing festival daies, but to instruct the people in the wayes of Godliness.*].

Answ. Socrates plainly rebuketh the busie Ceremonious arrogancy of after Ages, for making new holy dayes; and doth not at all mean the Lords day; but saith that to make *festivals*, that is, other and more, as since they did, was none of the Apostles business. Nor is this any thing at all to the matter of fact, which none denyed.

16. I will add that as another Testimony which *p. 9.* he citeth against it. The Council at *Paris, An.* 829. *c.* 50. which as he speaketh ascribeth the keeping of the Lords day to *Apostolical Tradition, confirmed by the Authority of the Church*: The words are [*ut creditur Apostolorum traditione, immo Ecclesiæ authoritate descendit,*&c.] Now I have proved that if the Apostles did it, they did it by the Holy Ghost, and by Authority from Christ,

But he citeth *p.* 7, 8. the words of *Athanasius, Maximus Taurinensis* and *Augustine*, saying
that

that [*We honour the Lords day for the Resurrection, and because Christ rose, and* (**Aug.**) *The Lords day was declared to Christians by the Resurrection of our Lord, and from that (or from him rather) began to have its festivity*] From whence he gathereth that it was only done by the authority of the Church and not by any precept of our Saviour.

Answ. As if Chrifts Refurrection could not be the fundamental occafion, and yet Chrifts Law the obliging caufe? Would any elfe have thus argued, [*The Jews observed the seventh day Sabbath, because the Creator rested the seventh day: Therefore they had no command from God for it?*] Woe to the Churches that have fuch expofitors of Gods commands! Or as if Chrift who both Commiffioned and Infpired the Apoftles by the Holy Ghoft, to teach all his commands, and fettle Church Orders, were not thus the chief Author of what they did by his *Commiffion* and *Spirit*: What *Church* can fhew the like Commiffion or the like Miraculous and Infallible Spirit as they had?

See further *Auguft. de Civitat. Dei l.* 22. *c.* 30. *& Serm.* 15. *de Verb. Apoftol.*

But, faith he, *Chrift and two of his Difciples travelled on the day of his Refurrection from* Jerufalem *to* Emaus, *feven miles, and back again, which they would not have done if it had been a Sabbath.*

Answ. 1. They would not have done it if it had been a Jewifh Sabbath of Ceremonial Reft; But thofe that you count too precife will go as far now in Cafe of need to hear a Sermon: And remember that they spent the time in Chrifts preaching and their Hearing and Conferring after of it. 2. But we grant that though the Foundation was laid by Chrifts Refurrection, yet it was not a Law fully promulgate to, and underftood by the Apoftles till the *Coming down of the Holy Ghoft* (nor many greater matters neither) who was *promifed* and *given* to *teach them all things* &c.

And it is worth the noting how *Heylin* beginneth his Chap. 3 l. 2. [*The Lords day taken up by the common confent of the Church, not inftituted or eftablifhed by any Text of Scripture, or Edict of Emperour, or Decree of Council, fave that fome few Councils did reflect upon it: In that which follows we fhall find both Emperours and Councils very frequent in ordering things about this day and the Service of it.*]

Anfw. Note Reader, What could poffibly befides Chrift and the Holy Ghoft in the Apoftles be the Inftituter of a day, which neither *Emperour* nor *Council* inftituted, and yet was received by the *common confent of all Churches in the World*, even from *and in the Apoftles dayes?* Yea, as this man confeffeth *by their Approbation and Authority?*

But hence forward in the fourth Century I am prevented from bringing in my moft numerous witneffes, by *Heylins* Confeffion that now Emperours, Councils and all were for it. But yet let the Reader remember, 1. How few and fmall Records be left of the *fecond Century*, and not many of the *third*. 2. And that Hiftorical copious Teftimonies of the fourth Century, that is Emperours, Councils, and the moft pious and
learned

learned Fathers, attesting that the Universal Church received it from the Apostles, is not vain or a small Evidence; when as the fourth Century began but 200 years after St. *Johns* death, or within less than a year.

And that the first Christian Emperour finding all Christians unanimous in the possession of the day, should make a Law (as our Kings do) for the due observing of it; And that the first General Council should establish uniformity in the very Gesture of Worship on that day, are strong Confirmations of the matter of fact, that the Churches unanimously agreed in the holy use of it as a separated day even *from and in the Apostles dayes.*

Obj. But the Emperour Constantines *Edict alloweth Husbandmen to labour.*

Answ. Only in case of apparent hazard lest the fruits of the Earth be *lost*; as we allow Seamen to work at Sea, in case of necessity. And so though by his second Edict Manumission was allowed to the Judges as an act of Charity, yet they were forbidden Judging in all other ordinary causes, lest the day be profaned by wranglings.

Gratian, Valentinian, and *Theodosius* by their Edict forbad publick spectacles or shews on the Lords day. And all seeking and judging of Debts and litigious Suits. And afterward *Valentinian* and *Valens* make an Edict that no *Christian should on that day be convented by the Exactors or Receivers.*

Ob. But (saith H.) for 300. years there was no Law to bind men to that day.

Answ.

Answ. The Apostles Institution was a Law of Christ by his spirit, *Mat.* 28. 20. And how should there be a humane Law before there was a Christian Magistracie?

Obj. Saith H. p. 95. *The powers which raised it up, may take it lower if they please, yea take it quite away,* &c.

Ans. True: that is, Christ may: And when he doth it by himself, or by new Apostles, who confirm their Commission by Miracles, we will obey: But we expect his presence with the Apostolical constitutions to the end of the World, *Mat.* 28. 20.

Theodosius also enacted that on the Lords day and in the *Christmas,* and on *Easter* and to *Whitsuntide* the publike Cirques and Theaters should be shut up. (For we grant that when Christian Magistrates took the matter in hand, other Holy dayes were brought in by degrees; whereas before the Christians indeed met (yea and Communicated) as oft as they could, even most daies in the week; but did not separate the daies as holy to Gods service as they did the Lords day: Only *Christmas* day, and the Memorials of those Martyrs that were neer them (to encourage the people to constancy) they honoured somewhat early; But those were *anniversary,* and not *weekly.* And the *Wednesdays,* and *Fridays,* were kept by them but as we keep them now, or as a Lecture-day.

I grant also that when Christian Magistracie arose, as the Holy dayes multiplied, the manner of the dayes observation altered. For whereas from the *beginning,* the Christians used to stay together

together from *morning till night*, (partly through *devotion*, and partly for fear of *persecution*, if they were noted to go in and out;) Afterward being free, they met twice a day, with intermission as we do now. Not that their whole dayes Service was but an hour or two as *Heylin* would prove from a perverted word of *Chrysostomes* and another of *Origenes* (or *Ruffinus*) and from the length of their published Homilies: For he perverteth what was spoken of the length of the *Sermon*, as spoken of the length of all the *Service of the whole day*: whereas there was much more time spent in the *Eucharistical* and *Liturgick* offices, of Prayer, Praise, Sacraments, and Exhortations proper to the Church, than was in the *Sermon*. When I was suffered to exercise my Ministry my self, having four hundred or five hundred if not six hundred to administer the Sacrament to (though twice the number kept themselves away) it took up the time of *two Sermons* usually to administer it, besides all the ordinary Readings, Prayers and Praises Morning and Evening.

Heylin noteth by the way, 1. That now officiating in a white garment begun; 2. And Kneeling at the Sacrament; which last he proveth from two or three words where *Adoration* only is named: But, 1. A late Treatise hath fully proved that the *White garment* was not a Religious Ceremony then at all, but the Ordinary *splendid Apparel* of honourable persons in those times, which were thought meet for the honour of the Ministry when Christian Princes did advance them. 2. And he quite forgot that Adoration on the

the Lords dayes was ever used *standing*, and that he had said before, that it was above a thousand years before the custome was altered.

The inclinations to overmuch strictness on the Lords day. The destruction of the Gothish Army by the Romans in *Africa* because they would not fight on that day, &c. see in *Heylin*, p. 112, 113, &c. His translation of the words of the Synod or Council at *Mascon*, 588. I think worthy the transcribing.

[" It is observed that Christian people do very
" rashly slight and neglect the Lords day ; giving
" themselves thereon as on other dayes, to conti-
" nual labours, &c. Therefore let every Christian,
" in case he carry not that name in vain, give eare
" to our instruction ; knowing that we have
" care that you should do well, as well as the
" power to bridle you, that you do not ill. It
" followeth, *Custodite Diem Dominicum qui nos*
" *denuo peperit,* &c. Keep the Lords day, the day
" of our new birth, whereon we were delivered
" from the snares of sin. Let no man meddle in
" Litigious Controversies, or deal in actions or
" Law suites ; or put himself at all on such an
" exigent, that needs he must prepare his Oxen
" for their daily work, but exercise your selves
" in Hymnes, and singing praises unto God ; be-
" ing intent thereon both in mind and body. If
" any have a Church at hand, let him go unto
" it, and there pour forth his soul in tears and
" Prayers ; his Eyes and Hands being all that
" day lifted up to God. It is the everlasting day
" of rest, insinuating to us under the shadow of
" the seventh day or Sabbath, in the Law and
" Prophets:

"Prophets: And therefore it is very meet that
"we should celebrate this day with one accord,
"whereon we have been made what at first we
"were not. Let us then offer to God our free
"and voluntary service, by whose great good-
"ness we are freed from the Goal of error: not
"that the Lord exacts it of us, that we should
"celebrate this day in a corporal abstinence or
"rest from labour, who only looks that we do
"yield obedience to his holy will, by which
"contemning earthly things, he may conduct
"us to the Heavens of his infinite mercy. How-
"ever if any man shall set at naught this our
"Exhortation, be he assured, that God shall
"punish him as he hath deserved; and that he
"shall be also subject unto the Censures of the
"Church. In case he be a Lawyer, he shall
"lose his cause; if that he be an Husbandman,
"or Servant, he shall be corporally punished for
"it: But if a Clergy-man or Monk, he shall be
"six Moneths separated from the Congrega-
"tion.]

His reproof of *Gregorius Turonensis* for his strictness for the Lords day, sheweth but his own dissent from him and from the Churches of that Age.

King *Alfreds* Laws for the observation of the Lords day, and against Dicing, Drinking, &c. on it, are visible in our own Constitutions, in *Spelman* and others. And many more Edicts and Laws are recited by *H.* himself of other Countreys.

Two are worthy the observation for the Reasons of them. 1. A Law of *Clotharius* King of
- *France,*

France, forbidding servile labours on the Lords day [*Because the Law forbids it, and the holy Scripture wholly contradicteth it.*] 2. A Constitution of the Emperour *Leo Philosophus*, to the same purpose [*Secundum quod Spiritui sancto ab ipsoq; institutis Apostolis placuit ; As it pleased the Holy Ghost and the Apostles instructed by him.*] You see that then Christian Princes judged the Lords day to be of Divine Institution. Yea, to these he addeth two more Princes of the same mind, confessing that *Leo* was himself a Scholar, and *Charles* the Great had as Learned men about him, as the times then bred, and yet were thus perswaded of the day ; yea, and that many Miracles were pretended in confirmation of it ; yet he affirmeth, that the *Church and the most learned men in it were of another mind.* Let us hear his proofs.

1. Saith he, *Isidore* a Bishop of *Sevil makes it an Apostolical Sanction only, no Divine Commandment : a day designed by the Apostles, for Religious Exercises in honour of our Saviours resurrection ; and it was called the Lords day therefore: to this end and purpose, that resting in the same from all earthly acts and the temptations of the world, we might intend Gods holy Worship, giving this day due honour for the hope of the resurrection which we have therein.* The same *verbatim* is repeated by *Beda l. de Offic.* and by *Raban. Maurus l. de inst. Chr. l. 2. c. 24.* and by *Alcuinus de Die Offic. c. 24. which plainly shews, that all these took it only for an Apostolical usage,* &c.

Answ. Reader, is not here a strange kind of proof ? This is but just the same that we assert, and

and I am proving; save that he most grosly puts an *Apostolical usage*, and *sanction* (*sanxerunt*) as distinct from, and exclusive of a *Command*, which I have fully proved to be Christs own Act and Law to us, by vertue of 1. Their Commission: 2. And the infallible Spirit given them.

And having brought the History to so fair an account by our chief Adversaries own Citations and confessions, I will not tire my self and the Reader with any more; but only wish every Christian to consider, whether they that thus distinguish between *Apostolical Sanctions*, and *Divine Institutions* as this man doth, do not teach men to deny all the holy Scriptures of the New Testament, as being but Apostolical writings: and go far to deny or subvert Christianity it self; by denying the Divine Authority of these Commissioned Inspired men, who are foundations of the Church, and sealed their Doctrine by Miracles, and from whom it is that our Christian Faith, and Laws, and Church constitutions which are Universal and Divine, are received.

I only remember you of *Pliny* a Heathens testimony, of the Christians practice *stato die*. No man can question *Pliny* on the account of Partiality: And therefore though a Heathen, his Historical testimony as joyned with all the Christian Church History, hath its credibility. He telleth *Trajan*, that it was the use of Christians *on a stated day, before it was light to meet together, to sing a Hymn to Christ as to God* secum invicem, *among themselves by turns; and to bind themselves by a Sacrament, not to do any wickedness, but that they commit not Thefts, Robberies, Adulteries,*

teries; that they break not their word (or trust) that they deny not the pledge (or pawn); which being ended they used to depart, and to come again together to take meat, but promiscuous and harmless.] Epist. 97. p. 306, 307.

Where note, 1. That by a *stated day*, he can mean no other than the *Lords day*, as the consent of all other History will prove. 2. That this is much like the testimonies of *Justin* and *Tertullian*, and (supposing what they say of the use of Reading the Scripture, and Instructing the Church) it sheweth that their chief work on that day, was the Praises of God for our Redemption by Christ, and the celebration of the Lords Supper; and the Disciplinary exercises of Covenanters thereto belonging. 3. That they had at that time where *Pliny* was two meetings that day, that is, they went home, and came again to their Feast of Love, in the Evening. (Which, no doubt, was varied, as several times, and places, and occasions required; sometimes departing and coming again, and sometimes staying together all day.) 4. That this Epistle of *Pliny* was written in *Trajans* dayes, and it is supposed in his second year: And *Trajan* was Emperour the year that St. *John* the Apostle died, if not a year before; so that it is the Churches custom in the end of the Apostles dayes, which *Pliny* here writeth of. 5. That he had the fullest testimony of what he wrote, it being the consent of the Christians whom he, as Judge, examined; even of the timorous that denyed their Religion, as well as of the rest. And many of them upon his prohibition forbore these meetings.

meetings. 6. And the number of them he telleth *Trajan* in City and Countrey was great, of persons of all degrees and ranks.

So that when 1. Christian History, 2. And Heathen, acquaint us with the matter *of fact*, that the day was kept in the Apostles time; 3. Yea, when no Hereticks or Sects of Christians are found contradicting it, but the Churches then and after universally practised it without any controversie; what fuller historical evidence can there be? And to say, that 1. The Apostles would not have reproved this, if it had not been their own doing: 2. Or that it could be done, and they not know it: 3. And that all Christians who acknowledged their authority, would have consented in such a practice superstitiously before their faces, and against their wills, and no testimony be left us of one faithful Church or Christian that contradicted it, and stuck to the Apostolical authority, even where the Churches received their writings, and publickly read them; all this is such, as is not by sober Christians to be believed.

But the great Objection will be, *That other things also were then taken for Apostolical Traditions, and were customs of the universal Church, as well as this; which things we now renounce as superstitious.*

Answ. Though I answered this briefly before, I now give you this fuller answer: I. It is but few things that come under this charge, *viz.* the Unction, white Garment, with the taste of Milk and Honey at Baptism, Adoration towards the East, and that standing; and not kneeling on the Lords

Lords dayes, and the Anniverſary Obſervation of *Eaſter* and *Whitſuntide*: And the laſt is but the keeping of one or two Lords dayes in the year with ſome note of diſtinction from the reſt, ſo far as there was any agreement in it. 2. That theſe are not uſually by the Antients called Apoſtolical Traditions, but *Cuſtoms of the Univerſal Church*: 3. That when they are called *Traditions* from the Apoſtles, it is not with any aſſertion that the Apoſtles inſtituted them, but that they are ſuppoſed to be from their times, becauſe their Original is not known. 4. That the Antients joyn not the Lords day with theſe, but take the Lords day for an Apoſtolical inſtitution written in Scripture, though the univerſal practice of all Churches fuller deliver the certain Hiſtory of it: But the reſt they take for *unwritten Cuſtoms*, as diſtinct from Scripture Ordinances. (As *Epiphanius* fully ſheweth.) 5. That moſt Chriſtians are agreed, that if theſe later could be proved Apoſtolical Inſtitutions for the Church univerſal, it would be our duty to uſe them, though they were not in Scripture. So that we reject them only for want of ſuch proof: But the proof of the Lords dayes ſeparation being far better (by concurrence of Scripture and all antient Hiſtory) it followeth not that we muſt doubt of that which hath full and certain proof, becauſe we muſt doubt of that which wants it. 6. And if it were neceſſary that they ſtood or fell together (as it is not) it were neceſſary that we did receive thoſe three or four Ceremonies, for the ſake of the Lords day, which hath ſo great evidence, rather than that we caſt
off

off the Lords day, becaufe of thefe Ceremonies. Not only becaufe there is more Good in the Lords day, than there is evil to be any way fufpected by a doubter in thefe Ceremonies; but efpecially becaufe the Evidence for the day is fo great, that it the faid Ceremonies had but the fame, they were undoubtedly of Divine authority or inftitution. In a word, I have fhewed you fomewhat of the evidence for the Lords day; Do you now fhew me the like *for them*, and then I will prove that both muft be received: But if you cannot, do not pretend a parity. 7. And the fame Churches laying by the *Cuftoms* aforefaid, or moft of them, did fhew that they took them not indeed for Apoftolical inftitutions, as they did the Lords day which they continued to obferve; not as a Ceremony, but as a neceffary thing. 8. And the ancient Churches did believe, that even in the Apoftles dayes fome things were ufed as Indifferent which were mutable, and were not Laws, but temporary cuftoms. And fome things were neceffary, fetled by Law for perpetuity: Of the former kind they thought were, the greeting one another with a holy kifs, the Womens praying covered with a Veil, (of which the Apoftle faith, that it was then and there fo decent, that the contrary would have been unfeemly, and the Churches of God had no fuch cuftom, (by which he anfwereth the contentious) yet in other Countreys, where cuftom altereth the fignification, it may be otherwife: Alfo that a man wear not long hair; and that they have a Love Feaft on the Lords day, (which yet *Paul* feemeth to begin

to

to alter in his rebuke of the abusers of it, 1 *Cor.* 11.) And if these ancient Churches thought the Milk and Honey, and the white Garment, and the Station and Adoration Eastwards, to be also such like indifferent mutable customs, as it is apparent they did, this is nothing at all to invalidate our proof, that the Lords day was used (and consequently appointed) in the dayes of the Apostles.

Obj. *At least it will prove it mutable as they were.*

Answ. No such matter: Because the very nature of such Circumstances, having no stated necessity or usefulness, sheweth them to be mutable. But the reason of the Lords dayes use is perpetual: And it is founded partly in the Law of nature, which telleth us that some stated dayes should be set apart for holy things; and partly in the positive part of the fourth Commandment; which telleth us, that *once* God *determined of one day in seven*, yea, and this upon the ground of his own Cessation of his Creation-work, that man on that day might observe a Holy Rest in the worshipping of the great Creator, which is a Reason belonging not to the Jews only, but to the whole world. Yea, and that Reason (whatever Dr. *Heylin* say to the contrary, from the meer silence of the former History in *Genesis*) doth seem plainly to intimate that this is but the repetition of that Law of the Sabbath which was given to *Adam*: For why should God begin two thousand years after to give men a Sabbath upon the reason of his rest from the Creation, and for the Commemoration

tion of it, if he had never called man to that Commemoration before.

And it is certain that the Sabbath was observed at the falling of Manna before the giving of the Law: And let any considerate Christian judge between Dr. *Heylin* and us in this; 1. Whether the not *falling of Manna,* or the *Rest of God* after the Creation, was like to be the Original reason of the Sabbath. 2. And whether if it had been the *first*, it would not have been said, *Remember to keep holy the Sabbath day; for on six dayes Manna fell, and not on the seventh,*] rather than [*For in six dayes God created Heaven and Earth, &c. and rested the seventh day.*] And it is causally added, [*Wherefore the Lord blessed the Sabbath day and hallowed it.*] Nay, consider whether this annexed Reason intimate not, that the day on this ground being hallowed before, therefore it was that God sent not down the Manna on that day, and that he prohibited the people from seeking it.

And he that considereth the brevity of the History in *Genesis,* will think he is very bold, that obtrudeth on the world his Negative Argument: [*The Sabbath is not there mentioned: therefore it was not then kept.*]

And if it was a *Positive Law* given to *Adam* on the reason of the *Creation Rest*, it was then *such a Positive*, as must be *next* to a *Law of Nature*, and was given to all mankind in *Adam*, and *Adam* must needs be obliged to deliver it down to the world.

So that though the *Mosaical* Law (even as given in Stone) be ceased, yea, and *Adams* Positives

sitives too, formally as such; yet this is sure, that *once God himself determined by a Law, that one stated day in seven, was the fittest proportion of time to be separated to holy Worship.* And if it was so once, yea, to all the world from the Creation, it is so still: Because there is still the same reason for it: And we are bound to judge Gods determination of the proportion to be wiser than any that we can make. And so by parity of Reason consequentially even those abrogated Laws do thus far bind us still; not so far as abrogated; but because the record and reason of them, is still a signification of the due proportion of time, and consequently of our duty.

Now the Lords day, supposing one weekly day to be due, and being but that day determined of, and this upon the Reason of the Resurrection, and for the Commemoration of our Redemption, and that by such inspired and authorized persons, it followeth clearly, that this is no such mutable ceremony, as a Love Feast, or the Kiss of Love, or the Veil, or the washing of feet, or the anointing of the sick, which were mostly occasionall actions and customs taken up upon reasons proper to those times and places.

Obj. *But by the reason aforesaid, you will prove the continuance of the seventh day Sabbath; as grounded on the Creation rest.*

Answ. This is anon to be answered in due place. I only prove that it continued, till a successive dispensation, and Gods own change did put an end to it; but no longer.

Obj. *But to commemorate the Creation, and praise*

praise the Creator is a Moral work, and therefore ceaseth not.

Answ. True: but that it be done on the *seventh day*; is that which ceaseth. For the *same work* is transferred to the *Lords day*; and the *Creator and Redeemer* to be honoured together in our Commemoration. For the *Son* is the only way to the Father; who hath restored us to Peace with our Creator; And as no man cometh to the Father but by the Son, and as we must not now worship God, as a Creator and Father never offended, but as a Creator and Father reconciled by Christ, so is it the appointment of Christ by the Holy Ghost, that we commemorate the work of Creation now as repaired and restored by the work of Redemption, on the Lords day, which is now separated to these works.

That the Sabbath was appointed to *Adam*, *Wallæus* on the fourth Commandment, *cap.* 3. and *Rivet differt. de sab. c.* 1. have most copiously proved. And *Clem. Alex. Strom. l.* 5. out of *Homer, Hesiod, Callimachus* and others proveth that the Heathens knew of it.

We may therefore summ up the prerogatives of the Lords day, as *Leo* did, *Ep.* 81. *c.* 1. *On this day the world began; on this day by Christs Resurrection, Death did receive Death, and Life its beginning; on this day the Apostles take the trumpet of the Gospel to be preached to all Nations; on this day the Holy Ghost came from the Lord to the Apostles,* &c. See more in *Athanas. de Sab. & Circ. & August. Serm.* 154. *de Tempore.* Therefore saith *Isychius in Levit. l.* 2. *c.* 9. *The Church setteth apart the Lords day for holy Assemblies.*

And in the times of Heathenish persecution, when men were asked, *Whether they were Christians, and kept the Lords dayes*, they answered that *they were, and kept the Lords day*, which Christians must not omit: as you may see *Act. Martyr. apud Baron. an.* 303. *n.* 37, 38, 39. They would die rather than not keep the holy assemblies and the Lords dayes: For saith *Ignatius, After the Sabbath every lover of Christ celebrateth the Lords day consecrated to* (or by) *the Lords resurrection, the Queen and chief of all dayes* (as is afore cited.) For saith *Augustine, The Lords Resurrection hath promised us an eternal Day, and consecrated to us the Lords day; which is called the Lords, and properly belongeth to the Lord, Serm.* 15. *de Verb. Apost.* And saith *Hilary Proleg. in Psalm. Though the name and observance of a Sabbath was placed to the seventh day, yet is it the eighth day, which is also the first, on which we rejoyce with the perfect festivity of the Sabbath.*

Of the full keeping of the whole day, and of the several Exercises in which it was spent, and of the more numerous testimonies of Antiquity hereupon, Dr. *Young* in his *Dies Dominica* hath said so much, with so much evidence and judgement, that I purposely omit abundance of such Testimonies, because I will not do that which he hath already done; The Learned Reader may there find unanswerable proof, of the matter of fact, that the Lords day was kept in the Apostles dayes, and ever since as by their appointment; And for the unlearned Reader, I fear lest I have too much interrupted him with Citations already.

dy. I only tell him in the Conclusion, that *If Scripture History interpreted and seconded by fullest practice and History of all the Churches of Christ, and by the consent of Heathens and Hereticks, and not contradicted by any Sect in the world, be to be believed, then we must say, that the Lords day was commonly kept by the Christians in and from the Apostles times.*

Prop. 11. *This evidence of the Churches universal constant usage, is a full and sufficient proof of the matter of fact, that it was a day set apart by the Apostles for holy Worship, especially in the publick Church-assemblies.*

1. It is a full proof, that such *Assemblies were held on that day above others, as a separated day.* For if it was the usage in *Anno* 100. (in which the Apostle *John* dyed) it must needs be the usage in the year 99. in which he wrote his Revelations, where he calleth it the *Lords day*: For all the Churches could not silently agree on a sudden to take up a new day, without debate and publick notice, which could not be concealed. And if it was the universal usage in the dayes of *Ignatius* or *Justin Martyr*, it was so also in the dayes of St. *John*, (and so before) For the Churches were then so far disperfed over the world, that it would have taken up much time to have had Councils and meetings or any other means for agreement on such things.

And it is utterly improbable that there would have been no dissenters? For, 1. Did *no Christians* in the world so neer to the Apostles daies make any scruple of *superstition*? or of such an addition

to

to Divine institutions? 2. Was there no Countrey, nor no persons whose *interest* would not better suit with another day, or an uncertain day? or at least their *opinions?* when we find it now so hard a matter to bring men in one Countrey, to be all of one opinion. 3. And there was then no *Magistrate* to *force* them to such an Union; And therefore it must be *voluntary*. 4. And they had in the *second age* such Pastors as the *Apostles themselves* had *ordained*, and as had conversed with them, and been trained up by them and knew their mind, and cannot soberly be thought likely to consent all on a sudden to such a new institution, without and contrary to the Apostles sense and practice. 5. Yea, they had yet Ministers that had that *extraordinary spirit* which was given by the laying on of the Apostles hands: For if the *aged Apostles* ordained *young men*, it is to be supposed that most of those young men, (such as *Timothy*) overlived them. 6. Yea and the *ordinary Christians* in those times had those *extraordinary gifts* by the laying on of the Apostles hands, as appeareth evidently in the case of *Samaria*, Act. 8. and of the Corinthians, 1 *Cor.* 12. & 14. and of the Galathians, *Gal.* 3. 1, 2, 3. And it is not to be suspected that all these *inspired Ministers* and *people* would consent to a superstitious innovation, without and against the Apostles minds.

2. Therefore this history is a full proof, that these things *were done by the consent and appointment of the Apostles.* For, 1. As is said, the inspired persons and Churches could not so suddenly be brought to *forsake them universally* in such

such a case. 2. The Churches had all so high an *esteem* of the Apostles, that they took their Authority for the highest, and their judgement for *infallible*, and therefore received their writings as *Canonical and Divine*. 3. The Churches professed to observe the Lords day as an *Apostolical Ordinance*, And they cannot be all supposed to have conspired in a *lie*, yea to have *belyed the Holy Ghost*. 4. The *Apostles themselves* would have controlled this course, if it had not been by their own appointment. For I have proved that the usage was in their *own daies*. And they were not so carelefs of the preservation of Christs Ordinances and Churches, as to let such things be done, without contradiction; when it is known how *Paul* strove to resist and retrench all the corruptions of Church-order in the Churches to which he wrote. If the Apostles, silently connived at such corruptions, how could we rest on their authority ? Especially the Apostle *John* in *an.* 99 would rather have written against it as the superstition of Usurpers (as he checkt *Diotrephes* for contempt of him) than have said that he *was in the Spirit on the Lords day* when he saw Christ, and received his Revelation and message to the Churches. 5. And if the Churches had taken up this practice universally without the Apostles, it is utterly improbable that no Church writer would have committed to memory either that *one Church* that begun the custome, or the *Council* or *means* used for a sudden Confederacy therein. If it had begun with *some one Church*, it would have been long before the rest would have been brought to an agreeing Consent. It was many hundred years before they all agreed of the Time of *Easter*; And it was till the middle of *Chrysostomes sometimes* time (for he saith it was but ten years agoe, when he wrote it) that they agreed of the time of Christs Nativity.

But if it had been done by Confederacy at once, the motion, the Council called about it, the debates, and the dissenters and resistances would all have been matter of fact, so notable, as would have found a place in some Author or Church History: Whereas there is not a Syllable of any such thing; either of Council, letter, messenger, debate, resistance, &c. Therefore it is evident that the thing was done by the Apostles.

Prop. 12. *They that will deny the validity of this Historical evidence, do by consequence betray the Christian faith, or give away or deny the necessary means of proving the truth of it, and of many great particulars of Religion.*

I suppose that in my Book called *The Reasons of the Christian Religion*, I have proved that Christianity is proved true, by the SPIRIT as the great witness of Christ, and of the Christian Verity; But I have proved withall, the necessity and certainty of historical means, to bring the matters of fact to our notice, as sense it self did bring them to the notice of the first receivers. For instance,

I. *Without such historical Evidence and Certainty*, we cannot be certain *what Books* of Scripture are *truly Canonical* and of *Divine authority*, and what not. This Protestants grant to Papists in the Controversie of Tradition. Though the Canon be it self compleat, and *Tradition is no supplement to make up the Scriptures*, as if they were *in suo genere imperfect*; yet it is commonly granted

granted that our Fathers and Teachers *Tradition* is the *hand* to deliver us this perfect Rule, and to tell us what parts make up the Canon.

If any say that the Books do prove themselves to be Canonical or Divine, I answer, 1. What man alive could tell without historical proof that the *Canticles*, or *Esther*, are Canonical? yea or *Ecclesiastes*, or the *Proverbs*, and not the Books of *Wisdome* and *Ecclesiasticus*?

2. How can any man know that the *Scripture histories* are Canonical? The suitableness of them to a holy soul, will do much to confirm one that is already holy, of the truth of the *Doctrines*: But if the spirit within us assure us immediately of the truth of the *History*, it must be by *Inspiration* and *Revelation*, which no Christians have, that ever I was yet acquainted with. For instance, that the Books of *Chronicles* are Canonical, or the Book of *Esther*, or the Books of the *Kings*, or *Samuel*, or *Judges*. And how much doth the *doctrine* of Christianity depend on the *history*? As of the *Creation*, of the Israelites bondage, and deliverance, and the giving of the Law, and *Moses* miracles, and of Chronologie and Chrifts Genealogie; and of the History of Chrifts own Nativity, Miracles and Life; and the History of the Apostles afterward? To say that the very History so far proveth its own truth, as that without subsequent History we can be sure of it, and must be, is to reduce all Chrifts Church of right believers into a narrow room; when I never knew the man that (as far as I could perceive) did know the History to be Divine by its proper evidence, without Tradition, and subsequent History. 3. And

3. And how can any man know the *Ceremonial Law* to be Divine, by its proper evidence alone? Who is he that readeth over *Exodus*, *Leviticus* and *Numbers*, that will say that without knowing by History that this is a Divine Record, he could have certainly perceived by the Book it self, that all these were indeed *Divine institutions* or *Laws*?

4. And how can any *meer Positive* institutions of the New Testament be known *proprio lumine*, by their own evidence to be Divine? As the institution of Sacraments, Officers, Orders, &c. What is there in them that can infallibly prove it to us?

5. And how can any *Prophecies* be known by their own evidence to be *Divine*, (till they are fulfilled and that shall prove it.)

I know that the *whole frame* together of the *Christian Religion* hath its *sufficient Evidence*, but we must not be guilty of a peevish rejecting it. The *Moral* part hath its witness *within us*, in that state of holiness which it imprinteth on the soul; and the rest are witnessed to, or proved partly *by that*, and partly *by Miracles*, and those and the records by *historical* evidence. But when God hath made *many things* necessary to the *full evidence*, and wranglers through partiality and Contention against each others will some throw away one part and some another, they will all prove destroyers of the faith (as all dividers be.) If the Papist will say, It is *Tradition* and not *inherent Evidence*, or if others will say that it is *inherent evidence alone*, and not *history or Tradition*, where God hath made both needful hereunto

unto, both will be found injurious to the faith.

II. Without this *historical* evidence we cannot prove that any of the books of Scripture are not *maimed* or *depraved*. That they come to our hands as the Apostles and Evangelists wrote them, uncorrupted. It is certain by History, that many Hereticks *did deprave* and *corrupt* them, and would have obtruded those Copies or Corruptions on the Churches: And how we shall certainly prove that they did not prevail, or that *their copies* are *false*, and *ours* are *true*, I know not without the help of History. *Mahomet* and his followers (more numerous than the Christians) pretend that *Mahomets* name was in the Gospel of *John* as the *Paraclet* or *Comforter* promised by Christ, and that the Christians have blotted it out, and altered the Writings of the Gospel. And how shall we disprove them but by Historical Evidence? As the Arrians, and Socinians pretend that we have added, 1 *John* 5. 7. for the Trinity, so others say of other Texts; And how shall we confute them without Historical Evidence?

III. Therefore we cannot make good the Authority of *any one single Verse or Text* of Scripture which we shall alledge, without *historical* evidence. Because we are not certain of that *particular text*, (or *words*,) whether it have been altered or added, or corrupted, by the fraud of Hereticks, or the partiality of some Christians, or the oversight of Scribes: For if a *Custome* of setting apart one day weekly, even the first, for publick Worship, might creep into all the Churches in the World, and no man know how, nor when;

when; much more might one or a few corrupt Copies become the exemplar of those that follow. For, *what day* all the Churches meet, men, women, and children know; Learned and unlearn'd know; the Orthodox and Hereticks know; and they *so know*, as that they *cannot choose* but know. But the alterations of a *Text*, may be unknown to all save the *Learned*, and the *observing diligent part* of the learned only, and those that they tell it to. And besides *Origen* (called a Heretick) and *Hierome*, alas, how few of the Fathers were able and diligent Examiners of such things? Therefore in the case of various Readings (such as *Ludov. Capellus* treats of in his *Critica Sacra*, contradicted in many things by Bishop *Usher* and others,) who are those Divines that have hitherto appealed either to the *Spirit*, or to the *proper light of the words*, for a decision? Who is it that doth not presently fly to *historical evidence*? And what that cannot determine we all confess to be uncertain? And if Copies and History had delivered to us as various Readings of *every Text* as they have done of *some*, every Text would have remained uncertain to us.

Let none say that this leaveth the *Christian Religion*, or the *Scriptures* uncertain: I have fully answered that elsewhere. 1. *Christian Religion*, that is, The *Material parts* of the Scripture on which our *salvation lyeth*, hath much fuller evidence, than *each particular Text* or *Canonical Book* hath. And we need not regard the perverse zeal for the Scriptures of those men that would make all our Christianity as uncertain, as the authority of a *particular Text* or *book* is. And therefore

therefore God in mercy hath so ordered it, that a thousand Texts may be uncertain to us, or not understood (no not by any or many Divines) and yet the *Christian faith* be not at all shaken, or ever the more uncertain for this: When as he that understandeth not or believeth not every essential Article of the faith, is *no Christian*. 2. And those *books* and *Texts* of Scripture, are fully certain by the *subservient help* of *History* and *usage*, which would be *uncertain* without them. Therefore it is the act of an enemy of the Scriptures, to cast away, and dispute against that *History* which is necessary to our knowledge of its *certainty*, and afterwards to plead that they who take in those necessary helps *do make it uncertain*: Even as if they should go about to prove that *all writings* are uncertain, and therefore that they make Christs doctrine uncertain, who rest upon the credit of writings, that is, the Sacred Scriptures.

IV. Without historical notice, how should we know that these Books were written by any of the same men that bear their names? As *Matthew, Mark, Luke, John, Paul, Peter,* &c. Especially when the Hereticks did put forth the Gospel of *Thomas, Nicodemus,* the Itinerary of *Peter* and many Books under venerable names? Or when the name of the Author is not notified to all Christians certainly, either by the spirit within us, or by the matter? And though our salvation depend not on the notice of the Penman, yet it is of great moment in the matter of faith.

F V. And

V. And how should we be certain that *no other Sacred Books* are lost, the knowledge of which would tell us of that which *these* contain not, and would help us to the better understanding of these? I know that a *priore* we may argue from Gods Goodness, that he will not so forsake his Church, As a Jew might have done before Christs incarnation, that the Gospel should be *written*, because it is best for the world or Church. But when we consider how much of the world and Church, God hath forsaken, since the Creation, and how dark we are in such Prognosticks, and how little we know what the Churches sins may provoke God to, we should be less confident of such reasonings, than we are of Historical Evidence, which tells us *de facto* what God hath done. So much of the use of the History, as to the Cause of the Scriptures themselves.

Next you may observe that the denyal of the certainty of humane History and usage, doth disadvantage Christianity in many great particular concernments. As, I. Without it we should not fully know whether *de facto* the Church and Ministry dyed, or almost dyed with the Apostles? And whether there have been any true Churches since then till our own dayes? Christs promise indeed tells us much; but if we had no History of the performance of it, we should be ready to doubt that it might be yet unperformed, as far as the promise to *Adam* (Gen. 3. 15.) and to *Abraham* (*in thy seed shall all the Nations of the earth be blessed*) were till the coming of Christ. Nor could we easily confute the *Roman* or any heretical Usurpation, which would pretend pos-
\hfill session

session since the Apostles daies, and that all that are since gone to Heaven, have gone thither by their way, and not by ours.

II. Nor could we much better tell *de facto*, whether Baptism have been administred in the form appointed by Christ, *In the name of the Father, of the Son, and of the Holy Ghost?* Indeed we may well and truly argue *a priore*, Christ commanded it, *Ergo* the Apostles obeyed him : But, 1. That Argument would hold good as to none or few but the Apostles: And, 2. It would as to them, be though true, yet much more dark than now it is, because, 1. We read that *Peter* disobeyed his command, in *Gal.* 2. And, 2. That after he had commanded them to Preach the Gospel to every Creature, and all the World, *Peter* scrupled still going to the Gentiles, *Act.* 10. And, 3. That when he said to them, *Pray thus* [*Our Father, &c.*] yet we never read that they after used that form of words ; so when he said to them [*Baptize in the name of the Father, &c.*] yet the Scripture never mentioneth that they or any other person, ever used that form of words. But yet usage and History assureth us that they did.

III. Nor have we any fuller Scripture proof, that the Apostles used to require of those that were to be Baptized any more than a general Profession of the substance of the Christian faith, in God the Father, the Son, and the Holy Ghost ; Or of the ancient use of the Christian Creed, either in the words now used, or any of the same importance. From whence many would inferr that any one is to be Baptized, who will but say, that [*I believe that Jesus Christ*

Christ is the Son of God] with the Eunuch, *Act.* 8. 37. or that Christ is come in the flesh, 1 *Joh.* 4. 2, 3.

But Historical evidence assureth us, that it was usual in those times, to require of men a *more explicite understanding profession* of the Christian faith before they were admitted to Baptisme; And that they had a summary or Symbole, fitted to that use, commonly called The Apostles Creed; at least as to the constant tenour of the matter, though some words might be left to the speakers will, and some little subordinate Articles may be since added. And that it was long after the use to keep men in the state of Catechised persons, till they understood that Creed. And it is in it self exceeding probable that though among the intelligent Jews, who had long expected the Messiah, the Apostles did Baptize thousands in a day, *Act.* 2. Yet where the Miraculous communication of the Spirit did not antecede (as it did *Act.* 10.) they would make poor Heathens who had been bred in ignorance to understand what they did first, and would require of them an understanding profession of their *Belief in God the Father, Son, and Holy Ghost*; which could not possibly (if understanding) contain much less than the *Symbolum fidei*, the Apostles Creed.

IV. Nor have we any Scripture proof, (except by inferring *obedience* from the precept) that ever the *Lords Prayer* was used in words, after Christ commanded or delivered it: Whence some inferr that it *should not* be so used: But Church History putteth that past doubt. Other such instances I pretermit.

I think now that I have fully proved to sober considerate Christians, that the matter of fact (that the *Lords day* was appointed by the Apostles peculiarly for Church-Worship) is certain to us by historical Evidence, added to the historical intimations in Scripture as a full exposition and confirmation of it: And that this is a proof that no Christian can deny without unsufferable injury to the Scriptures and the Christian cause.

CHAP. VI.

Prop. 5. *This Act of the Apostles appointing the Lords day for Christian Worship, was done by the special inspiration or guidance of the Holy Ghost.*

THis is proved, 1. Because it is one of those Acts or works of their Office, to which the Holy Ghost was *promised* them.

2. Because that such like or smaller things are by them ascribed to the Holy Ghost, Act. 15. 28. [*It seemed good to the Holy Ghost and us*] when they did but declare an antecedent duty, and decide a Controversie thereabout. See also, *Act.* 4. 8. *Act.* 5. 3. *&* 6. 3. with 7. 55. *Act.* 13. 2, 4. *&* 16. 6, 7. *&* 20. 23, 28. *&* 21. 11. 2 *Tim.* 1. 14. *Jud.* 20. *Act.* 11. 12, 28. *&* 19. 21. *&* 20. 22. 1 *Cor.* 5. 3, 4. *&* 14. 2, 15, 16. And 1 *Cor.* 7. 40. When *Paul* doth but counsel to a single life, he ascribeth it to the Spirit of God.

3. And

3. And if any will presume to say, that men purposely indued with the Spirit, for the works of their commission, did notwithstanding do such great things as this, without the conduct of that Spirit, they may by the same way of proceeding pretend it to be as uncertain, of every particular Book and Chapter in the New Testament, whether or no they wrote it by the Spirit: For if it be a sound inference, [*They had the promise and gift of the Spirit, that they might infallibly leave in writing to the Churches, the doctrines and precepts*, of Christ: Ergo *whatever they have left in Writing to the Churches as* the *doctrine* and *precepts* of Christ, is *Infallibly done by the Guidance of that Spirit,*] Then it will be as good an inference [*They had the promise and gift of the Spirit, that they might infallibly settle Church-orders for all the Churches universaly*: ergo, *Whatever Church-orders they setled for all the Churches universally, they setled them by the infallible guidance of that Spirit.*]

But this few Christians will deny, except some Papists, who would bring down Apostolical Constitutions to a lower rank and rate, that the Pope and his General Council may be capable of laying claim to the like themselves; and so may make as many more Laws for the Church as they please, and pretend such an authority for it as the Apostles had for theirs. By which pretense many would make too little distinction between Gods Laws, given by his Spirit, and the Laws of a Pope and Popish Council; and call them all but *The Laws of the Church*. Whereas there is no Universal Head of the Church but Christ,

Christ, who hath reserved Universal Legislation to Himself alone, to be performed by himself personally, and by his Advocate the Holy Ghost, in his Authorized and Infallibly-inspired Apostles, who were the Promulgators and Recorders of them; All following Pastors, being but (as the Jewish Priests were to *Moses* and the Prophets) the *preservers*, the *expositers*, and the *applyers* of that Law.

CHAP. VII.

Qu. 2. *Whether the seventh day Sabbath should be still kept by Christians, as of Divine obligation?* Neg.

I Shall here premise, That as *some superstition* is less dangerous than *prophaneness* (though it be *troublesome*, and have *ill consequents*,) so the Errour of them who keep *both daies* as of Divine appointment, is much *less* dangerous than theirs that keep *none*: yea and less dangerous, I think, than theirs who *reject* the Lords day, and keep the *seventh day* only. Because these latter are guilty of *two sins*, (the *rejecting of the right* day, and the keeping of the *wrong*; but the other are guilty but of *one* (the keeping of the *wrong* day.) Besides that if it were not done, with a superstitious conceit (that it is Gods Law) in some cases a day may be voluntarily set apart for holy duties, as daies of Thanksgiving and Humiliation now are.

But

But yet, though the rejecting of the Lords day be the greater fault (and I have no uncharitable censures of them that through weaknefs keep both daies) I muft conclude it as the truth, that *We are not obliged to the obfervation of the Saturday or feventh day as a Sabbath, or feparated day of holy Worfhip.*

Arg. 1. *That dayes obfervation which we are not obliged to, either by the Law of Nature, the Pofitive Law given to Adam, the Pofitive Law given to Noah, the Law of Mofes, nor the Law of Chrift incarnate, we are not obliged to by any Law of God* (as diftinct from humane Laws:) *But fuch is the obfervation of the feventh day as a Sabbath: Ergo we are not obliged to the obfervation of the feventh day as a Sabbath by any Law of God.*

The Minor I muft prove by parts. (For I think none will deny the fufficient enumeration in the Major.)

And, 1. That the Law of Nature bindeth us not to the feventh, or any one day of the feven more than other, appeareth, 1. In the *nature* and *reafon* of the *thing:* There is nothing in *nature* to evidence it to us to be Gods will. 2. By every *Chriftians experience:* No man findeth himfelf convinced of any fuch thing by *meer nature.* 3. By all the *Worlds experience:* No man can fay that a man of that opinion can bring any cogent evidence or argument from *nature alone* to convince another, that the feventh day muft be the Sabbath. Nor is it any where received as a Law of *Nature,* but only as a *Tradition* among fome few Heathens, and as *Law pofitive* by the *Jews,* and fome *few Chriftians.* I am not foli-

citous

citous to profecute this argument any further; becaufe I can confent that *all they* take the *feventh day for the Sabbath*, who can prove it to be fo by *meer natural Evidence*: which will not be one.

II. That the *Pofitive Law* made to *Adam* (before or *after* the fall) or to *Noah*, bindeth not us to keep the feventh day as a Sabbath, is proved.

1. Becaufe we are under a more *perfect fubfequent Law*; which being in force, the former more *imperfect ceafeth*. As the force of the *Promife* of the Incarnation of Chrift is ceafed by *his incarnation*, and fo is the *precept* which bound men to believe that he fhould *de futuro* be incarnate; and the Law of *Sacrificing* (which *Abel* doubtlefs received from *Adam*, though one of late would make it to be but *will-worfhip*;) fo alfo is the *Sabbath day*, as giving place to the day in which our *Redemption* is primarily commemorated, as the imperfect is done away when that which is more perfect cometh.

2. Becaufe that the Law of Chrift containeth an exprefs revocation of the feventh day Sabbath, as fhall be fhewed anon.

3. Becaufe God never required *two dayes* in *feven* to be kept as holy: Therefore the *firft* day being proved to be of Divine inftitution, the ceffation of the *feventh* is thereby proved: For to keep *two dayes* is contrary to the command which they themfelves do build upon, which requireth us to fanctifie a Sabbath, and labour fix dayes.

4. And when it is not probable that moft or many *Infidels* are bound to *Adams* day, for want of notice (at leaft;) For no Law can bind
without

without promulgation (though I now pass by the question, how far a promulgation of a positive to our first Parents may be said to bind their posterity, that have no intermediate notice) It seemeth less probable that *Christians* should be bound by it, who have a more perfect Law promulgate to them.

5. Nor is it probable that Christ and his Apostles and all the following Pastors of the Churches would have passed by this Positive Law to *Adam*, without any mention of it, if our universal obligation had been thence to be collected. Nay I never yet heard a Sabbatarian plead this Law, any otherwise than as supposed to be implyed or exemplified in the fourth Commandment.

III. And that the fourth Commandment of *Moses* Law bindeth us not to the seventh day Sabbath is proved.

1. Because that *Moses* Law *never bound* any to it but the Jews, and those Proselites that made themselves inhabitants of their Land, or voluntarily subjected themselves to their policy. For *Moses* was *Ruler* of none but the Jews; nor a *Legislator* or *deputed officer* from God to any other Nation. The *Decalogue* was but part of the *Jewish Law*, if you consider it not as it is written in *Nature*, but in *Tables of Stone*: And the Jewish Law was given as *a Law* to no other people but to them. It was a *National Law*, as they were a *peculiar people and holy Nation*. So that even in *Moses* daies it bound no other Nations of the World. Therefore it needed not any *abrogation* to the *Gentiles*, but a *declaration* that it did not bind them. 2. The

2. The whole Law of *Moses* formally as such is *ceased* or *abrogated* by Christ. I say, *As such;* Because *Materially*, the same things that are in that Law, may be the *matter* of the Law *of Nature*, and of the Law of *Christ:* of which more anon. That the *whole Law* of *Moses as such* is abrogated, is most clearly proved, 1. By the frequent arguings of *Paul*, who ever speaketh of that Law as ceased without excepting any part, And Christ saith, *Luke* 16. 16. The Law and the Prophets were untill *John*, that is, were the chief doctrine of the Church till then, *Joh*. 1. 17. *The Law was given by* Moses, *but grace and truth cometh by Jesus Christ*. No Jew would have understood this, if the word [*Law*] had not contained the Decalogue. So *Joh.* 7. 19, 23. *Act.* 15. 5, 24. It was the *whole Law* of *Moses, as such* which *by Circumcision* they would have bound men to. *Gal.* 5. 3. The Gentiles are said *to sin without Law*, even when they broke the *Law of Nature*, meaning [*without the Law of* Moses] *Rom.* 2. 12, 14, 15, 16. In all these following places its not part but the *whole Law of* Moses, which *Paul* excludeth (which I ever acknowledged to the Antinomians, though they take me for their too great Adversary,) *Rom.* 3. 19, 20, 21, 27, 28, 31. & 4. 13, 14, 15, 16. & 5. 13. 20. & 7. 4, 5, 6, 7, 8, 16. & 9. 4, 31, 32. & 10. 5. *Gal.* 2. 16, 19, 21. & 3. 2, 10, 11, 12, 13, 19, 21, 24. & 4. 21. & 5. 3, 4, 14, 23. & 6. 13. *Eph.* 2. 15. *Phil.* 3. 6, 9. *Heb.* 7, 11, 12, 19. & 9. 19. & 10. 28. 1 *Cor.* 9. 21.

2. More particularly there are some Texts which *express* the cessation of the *Decalogue* as it was

was *Moses* Law, 2 Cor. 3. 3, 7, 11. *Not in Tables of Stone, but in fleshly tables of the heart*—— *But if the Ministration of death written and engraven in stones was glorious, so that the Children of* Israel *could not stedfastly behold the face of* Moses *for the glory of his Countenance, which was to be done away (or is done away.)* They that say the *Glory*, and not *the Law* is here said to be *done away*, speak against the plain scope of the Text : For the Glory of *Moses* face, and the glorious manner of deliverance ceased in a few daies, which is not the cessation here intended ; But (as Dr. *Hammond* speaketh it) [*that Glory and that Law so gloriously delivered is done away*] And this the eleventh verse fullyer expresseth [*For if that which is done away was glorious (or, by Glory,) much more that which remaineth is glorious*, or (*in glory*) so that as it is not only the *Glory*, but the *Glorious Law*, *Gospel* or Testament which is said to *remain*, so it is not only the *Glory*, but the *Law* which was delivered *by Glory* which is expressly said to be done away: And this is the Law which was written in Stone—— Nothing but partial violence can evade the force of this Text.

So Heb. 7. 11, 12. [*Under it (* the *Levitical Priesthood) the people received the Law*—— *And the Priesthood being changed there is made of necessity a change also of the Law.* 18. *For there is verily a disanulling of the Commandment going before, for the weakness and unprofitableness thereof. For the Law made nothing perfect ; but the bringing in of a better hope*—— 22. *By so much was* Jesus *made a surety of a better Testament*] In all this it is plain that it is the whole frame of the

Mosaical

Mosaical Law that is changed, and the New Testament set up in its stead.

Heb. 9. 18, 19. *Neither was the first Dedicated without blood; For when Moses had spoken every precept to all the people according to the Law, &c.* Here the Law which is before said to be changed is said to contain *Every Precept.*

And Eph. 2. 15. *It is the Law of Commandments contained in Ordinances,* which Christ abolished in his flesh; which cannot be exclusive of the chief part of that Law.

Obj. *This is the Doctrine of the Antinomians, that the Law is abrogated, even the Moral Law.*

Ans. It is the Doctrine of the true Antinomians that we are under no Divine Law, neither of *Nature* nor of *Christ*; But it is the Doctrine of *Paul* and all Christians, that the Jewish Mosaical Law as such is abolished.

Obj. *But do not all Divines say that the Moral Law is of perpetual obligation?*

Ans. Yes; Because it is Gods Law of Nature, and also the Law of Christ.

Obj. *But do not most say that the Decalogue written in stone, is the Moral Law and of perpetual obligation.*

Answ. Yes: for by the word [*Moral*] they mean [*Natural*,] and so take *Moral*, not in the large sense as it signifieth a Law *de moribus* as all *Laws* are whatsoever, but in a narrower sense as signifying, that which by *Nature* is of *Universal* and *perpetual* obligation. So that they mean not that it is perpetual as it is *Moses* Law and written in Stone formally, but as it is *Moral,* that is *Natural*. And they mean that *Materially* the Decalogue containeth the same Law which is

the

the Law of Nature, and therefore is *materially* still in force: But they still except certain points and circumstances in it, as the prefatory reason [*I am the Lord that brought thee out of the Land of Ægypt, &c.*] And especially this of the seventh day Sabbath.

Q.1. *How far then are we bound by the Decalogue?*

Answ. 1. As it is the Law of Nature; 2. As it is owned by Christ, and made part of his Law. Therefore no more of it bindeth directly, than we can prove to be either the Law of *Nature*, or the Law of *Christ*. 3. As it was once a Law of God to the Jews, and was given them upon a reason common to them with us or all mankind, we must still judge, that it was once a Divine determination of what is most meet, and an exposition of a Law of Nature, and therefore consequentially, and as that which intimateth by what God once commanded, what we should take for his will, and is most meet, it obligeth still. And so when the Law of Nature forbiddeth Incest, or too near marriages, and God once told the Jews what degrees were to be accounted too near, this being *once* a Law to them *directly*, is a *Doctrine* and *Exposition* of the *Law of Nature* still to us; and so is *consequentially a Law,* by parity of reason. And so we shall shew anon that it is by the fourth Commandment.

IV. *The Law of Christ bindeth us not to the observation of the seventh day Sabbath.* Proved.

1. Because it is proved that Christ abrogated *Moses* Law as such, and it is no where proved that

that he reassumed this, as a part of his own Law. For it is no part of the Law of *Nature* (as is proved) (which we confess now to be part of his Law.)

Object. *Christ saith, that he came not to destroy the Law and Prophets, but to fulfill them, and that a jot or tittle shall not pass till all be fulfilled.*

Answ. He is the end of the Law for righteousness to every one that believeth, Rom. 10. 4. *The Law was a Schoolmaster to bring us to Christ,* Gal. 3. 24. He hath therefore *fulfilled* the Law according to his word, by his incarnation, life, death and resurrection. It is past away, but not unfulfilled: And fulfilling it, is not destroying it. The ends of it are all attained by him: 2. And though having attained its end, it ceaseth *formally,* as *Moses* Law; yet *materially,* all that is of natural obligation continueth under another *form*; that is, as part of *his perfect Law.* Therefore as our childish knowledge is said, as *knowledge* to be *increased* and not done away, when we come to maturity; but as *childish* to be done away; so the Mosaical Jewish Law, as Gods *Law in general* is *perfected* by the cessation of the parts which were fitted to the state of bondage, and by addition of more perfect parts (The natural part of it is made a part of a better Covenant or frame:) But yet as *Mosaical* and *imperfect* it is abolished.

Briefly this much sufficeth for the answer of all the allegations, by which any would prove the continuation of *Moses* Law, or any part of it formally as such. I only add, That all *Moses* Law,

Law, even the Decalogue was *Political*, even Gods Law for the Government of that particular Theocratical Policy, as a Political body. Therefore when the Kingdom or Policy ceased, the Law as Political could not continue.

2. It is proved that Christ by his Spirit in his Apostles did institute *another day*. And seeing the Spirit was given them to bring his words to remembrance, and to enable them to teach the Churches all things whatsoever he commanded them, it is most probable that this was at first one of Christs own personal Precepts.

3. And to put all out of doubt, that neither the Law of Nature, nor any Positive Law, to *Adam*, *Noah*, or *Moses*, or by Christ doth oblige us to the seventh day Sabbath, it is expresly repealed by the Holy Ghost, Col. 2. 16. [*Let no man therefore judge you in meats or in drink, or in respect of an Holy day (or Feast) or of the New Moon, or of the Sabbaths, which are a shadow of things to come; but the body is of Christ.*] I know many of late say, that by *Sabbaths* here is not meant the *weekly Sabbath*, but only other Holy dayes, as *Monethly* or *Jubilee rests*: But 1. This is to limit without any proof from the word of God:: When God speaks of *Sabbaths* in *general* without exception, what is man that he should put in exceptions without any proof of Authority from God? By such boldness we may pervert all his Laws. Read Dr. *Young* upon this Text. 2. Yea, when it was the *weekly Sabbath*, which then was *principally* known by the Name of a *Sabbath*, above all other Festivals whatsoever,

ever, it is yet greater boldnefs without proof to exclude the *principal* part, from whence the reft did receive the name. 3. Befides the *Feafts* and *New Moons* being here named as diftinct from the Sabbath, are like to include fo much of the other feparated dayes, as will leave it ftill more unmeet to exclude the weekly Sabbath in t' Explication of that word [*Sabbaths*] where-fo many Feafts are firft diftinguifhed : *Ex his, inquit Grotius, hic funt Azyma dies omer, fcenopegia, dies ἱλασμοῦ.*

Obj. *But the Sabbath mentioned in the Decalogue could not be included.*

Anfw. This is fpoken without proof, and the contrary is before proved.

Obj. *By this you will make the Chriftian Sabbath alfo to be excluded. Is not the Lords day a Sabbath ?*

Anfw. I am here to fpeak but of the *name* ; of which I fay, that the common fenfe of the word *Sabbath* was, *a Day fo appointed to Reft, as that the bodily Reft of it, was a primary part of its obfervation, to be kept for it felf*; and fuch the Jewifh Sabbaths were. Though fpiritual Worfhip was then alfo commanded, yet the *corporal Reft* was more exprefly or frequently urged in the Law, and this not only fubordinately as an advantage to the fpiritual worfhip, but *for it felf*, as an immediate and moft vifible and notable part of Sabbatizing. Even as other Ceremonies under the Law were commanded, not only as doctrinal Types of things fpiritual, but as external Acts of Ceremonious operous obedience fuited to the Jews Minority, which is after called

called the *yoke which they and their Fathers were unable to bear*, Acts 15. Whereas the *Lords day* is appointed but as a *seasonable time* subserviently to the *spiritual work* of the day; And the *bodily Rest*, not required as *primary obedience* for *it self*, but only *for the spiritual work sake*: and therefore no bodily labour is now unlawful, but such as is a hinderance to the *spiritual work* of the day (or accidentally a *scandal* and *temptation* to others) whereas the breach of the *outward Rest* of the *Jews Sabbath*, was a *sin directly of it self*, without *hinderance* of, or *respect* to the spiritual Worship. So that the *first notion* and *sense* of a *Sabbath* in these dayes being (in common use) *A day of such Ceremonial Corporal Rest*, as the *Jewish Sabbath was*, the Lords day is never in Scripture called by that name; but the proper name is [*The Lords day.*] And the ancient Churches called it constantly by that name, and never called it the *Sabbath*, but when they spake Analogically by allusion to the Jews Sabbath; even as they called the holy Table, *the Altar*, and the Bread and Wine, *the Sacrifice*. Therefore it is plain, that *Paul* is to be understood of all *proper Sabbaths*, and not of the *Lords day*, which was then and long after distinguished from the *Sabbath*.

And this *Ceremonial Sabbatizing* of the *Jews* was so strict, that the *Ceremoniousness* made them the scorn of the Heathens, as appeareth by the derisions of *Horat. li.* 1. *sat.* 9. *Persius sat.* 5. *Juvenal. sat.* 6. *Martial. lib.* 4. and others: whereas they derided not the Christians for the *Ceremonious Rest*, but for their *Worship* on that day.

day. The *Lords* day being not called a *Sabbath* in the old sense then only in use, but *distinguished* from the Sabbath, cannot be meant by the Apostle in his exclusion of the *Sabbath*.

Obj. But *the Apostles then met in the Synagogues with the Jews on the Sabbaths; Therefore it is not those dayes that he meaneth here.* Col. 2. 16.

Answ. 1. You might as well say, that therefore he is not for the cessation of the *Jewish manner of Worship*, or *Communion with them in it*, because he met with them.

2. And you may as well say, that he was for the continuance of Circumcision and Purification; because he purified himself and circumcised *Timothy*.

3. Or that he was for the continuance of their other Feasts, in which also he refused not to joyn with them.

4. But *Paul* did not keep their Sabbaths formally as Sabbaths, but only take the advantage of their Assemblies, to teach them and convince them; and to keep an interest in them: And not scandalize them by an unseasonable violation and contradiction.

5. And you must note also, that the Text saith not [*Observe not Sabbath dayes*] but [*Let no man judge you*] that is, Let none take it for your sin, that you observe them not; nor do you receive any such Doctrine of the *necessity* of keeping the Law of *Moses*.] The case seemeth like that of *things strangled* and *blood*, which were to be forborn among the Jews while they were offensive, and the use of them hindred their conversion.

Obj. *But the ancient Christians did observe both dayes.*

Answ. 1. In the first Ages *they* did as the *Apostles* did ; that is, 1. They observed no day strictly as a *Sabbath* in the notion then in use : 2. They observed the *Lords day*, as a day set apart by the Holy Ghost for Christian Worship. 3. They so far observed the *Jews Sabbath* materially, as to avoid their scandal, and to take opportunity to win them.

2. But those that lived far from all Jews, and those that lived after the Law was sufficiently taken down, did keep but *one day*, even the *Lords day*, as separated to holy uses : except some *Christians* who differed from the rest, as the followers of *Papias* did in the Millenary point.

3. And note that even these dissenters, did still make no question of keeping the *Lords day*, which sheweth that it was on foot from the times of the Apostles. So *Ignatius* (whoever it was, and whenever he wrote) saith that [*After the Sabbath we keep the Lords day.*] And *Pseudo-Clemens Can.* 33. saith [*Servants work five dayes, but on the Sabbath and Lords day, they keep holy day in the Church, for the Doctrine* (or Learning) *of Godliness*]

The Text of *Gal.* 4. 10. is of the same sense with *Col.* 2. 16. against the Jews Sabbath, and therefore needeth no other defence.

And I would have you consider, whether as Christs Resurrection was the foundation of the Lords day, so Christs lying dead and buried in a Grave on the seventh day Sabbath, was not a

funda-

fundamental abrogation of it : I say not the Actual and plenary abrogation : For it was the Command of Christ by his Word, Spirit, or both to the Apostles before proved, which fully made the change : But as the Resurrection was the Ground of the new day, so his Burial seemeth to intimate, that the day with all the Jewish Law which it was the symbolical profession of, lay dead and buried with him. Sure I am that he saith, when the Bridegroom is taken from them, then shall they fast and mourn; but he was most notably taken from them, when he lay dead in the Grave; And if they must *fast* and mourn that day, they could not keep it as a Sabbath, which was a day of joy. Therefore as by death he overcame him that had the power of death, *Heb.* 2. 14. and as he nailed the hand-writing of Ordinances to his Cross; so he buried the Sabbath in his Grave, by lying buried on that day.

And therefore the Western Churches, who had fewer Jews among them, did *fast* on the Sabbath day, to shew the change that Christs burial intimated : Though the Eastern Churches did not, lest they should offend the Jews.

And that the ancient Christians were not for sabbatizing on the seventh day, is visible in the writings of most, save the Eastern ones before mentioned. *Tertull. cont. Marcion li.* 1. *cap.* 20. *& Chrysost. Theodoret, Primasius, &c.* on *Gal.* 4. expound that Text, as that by *Dayes* is meant the Jewish Sabbath, and by Moneths, the New Moons, *&c.*

Cyprian 59. *Epist. ad Hidum* faith, that the *eighth day* is to *Christians*, what the *Sabbath* was to the *Jews*, and calleth the Sabbath, the Image of the Lords day. *Athanasius de Sab. & Circumcis.* is full and plain on it. See *Tertulian Advers. Judæ. c.* 4. *Ambros. in Eph.* 2. *August. Ep.* 118. *Chrysost. in Gal.* 1. *& Hom.* 12. *ad pop. Hilary* before cited *Prolog. in Psalm. Origen Hom.* 23. *in Num. Item Tertull. de Idol. c.* 14. *Epiphan. l.* 1. *num.* 30. noting the *Nazaræi* and *Ebionæi* Hereticks, that they kept the Jews Sabbath. In a word, The Council of *Laodicea* doth Anathematize them that did Judaize by forbearing their Labours on the Sabbath or seventh day. And as *Sozomen* tells us, that at *Alexandria* and *Rome* they used no Assemblies on the Sabbath, so where they did, in most Churches they communicated not in the Sacrament.

Yea, that *Ignatius* himself (true or false) who saith as aforecited [*After the Sabbath let every lover of Christ celebrate the Lords day*] doth yet in the same Epistle (*ad Magnes.*) before say [*Old things are passed away, behold all things are made new: For if we yet live after the Jewish Law, and the Circumcision of the flesh, we deny that we have received Grace ——— Let us not therefore keep the Sabbath (or sabbatize) Jewishly, as delighting in Idleness (or Rest from labour.) For he that will not labour, let him not eat. In the sweat of thy brows thou shalt eat thy bread.*] I confess I take the cited Texts to have been added since the body of the Epistle was written; but though the Writer savour of the Eastern custom, yet he sheweth they did not sabbatize on the account

count of the fourth Commandment, or supposed continuation of the Jewish Sabbath as a Sabbath: For bodily labour was strictly forbidden in the fourth Commandment.

Dionysius Alexandr. hath an Epistle to *Basilides* a Bishop on the Question, When the Sabbath Fast must end, and the observation of the Lords day begin, *Biblioth. Patr. Græc. Lat. Vol.* 1. *p.* 306. In which he is against them that end their Fast too soon. And plainly intimateth that the seventh day was to be kept, but as a preparatory Fast (being the day that Christ lay in the grave) and not as a Sabbath, or as the Lords day.

I cite not any of these, as a humane authority to be set against the authority of the fourth Commandment; But as the certain History of the change of the day which the Apostles made.

Qu. How far then is the fourth Commandment Moral? you seem to subvert the old foundation, which most others build the Lords day upon.

Answ. Let us not entangle our selves with the ambiguities of the word [*Moral*] which most properly signifieth *Ethical*, as distinct from *Physical*, &c. By *Moral* here is meant that which is (on what ground soever) of *perpetual* or *continued* obligation: And so it is all one as to ask how far it is still obligatory or in force; To which I answer,

1. It is a part of the *Law of Nature*, that *God be solemnly worshipped, in families and in holy assemblies.*

2. It is a part of the *Law of Nature*, that *where greater things do not forbid it, a stated time be appointed for this service, and that it be not left at Randome to every mans will.*

3. It is of the *Law of Nature*, that *where greater matters do not hinder it, this day be one and the same in the same Countreys; yea, if it may be through the world.*

4. It is of the *Law of Nature*, that *this day be not so rarely as to hinder the ends of the day, nor yet so frequently as to deprive us of opportunity for our necessary corporal labour.*

5. It is of the *Law of Nature*, that *the holy duties of this day be not hindered by any corporal work, or fleshly pleasure, or any unnecessary thing which contradicteth the holy ends of the day.*

6. It is of the *Law of Nature*, that *Rulers, and in special Masters of families, do take care that their inferiours thus observe it.*

In all these points the fourth Commandment being but a transcript of the *Law of Nature*, which we can yet prove from the *nature of the reason* of the thing, the *matter* of it continueth (not as Jewish, but) as *Natural*.

7. Besides all this, when no man of himself could tell, whether one day in *six* or *seven* or *eight* were his duty to observe, God hath come in, and 1. By *Doctrine* or *History* told us, that he *made the world in six dayes, and rested the seventh.* 2. By *Law*; and hath *commanded one day in seven to the Jews*; by which he hath made known *consequentially to all men, that one day in seven is the fittest proportion of time.* And the case being thus determined by God, by a *Law to others*, doth
con-

consequentially become a *Law to us*, because it is the determination of *Divine Wisdom*; unless it were done upon some reasons in which *their* condition *differeth* from *ours*. And thus the Doctrine and Reasons of an abrogated Law, continuing, may induce on us an obligation to duty. And in this sense the fourth Commandment may be said still to bind us to *one day in seven*.

But in two points the obligation (even as to the *Matter*) ceaseth. 1. We are not bound to *the seventh day*, because God our Redeemer who is Lord of the Sabbath, hath made a change. 2. We are not bound to a *Sabbath* in the *old notion*, that is, to a *day of Ceremonial Rest for it self required*; but to a day to be spent in *Evangelical Worship*.

And though I am not of their mind who say, that the *seventh day* is not commanded in the fourth Commandment, but a *Sabbath only*; yet, I think that it is evident in the words, that the *Ratio Sabbati*, and the *Ratio diei septimi* are distinguishable: And that the *Sabbath* as a *Sabbath*, is *first* in the precept, and the *particular day* is there but *secondarily*, and so *mutably*; as if God had said, *I will have a particular day set apart for a holy Rest, and for my Worship; And that day shall be one in seven, and the seventh also on which I rested from my works.*

And thus I have said as much as I think needful to satisfie the considerate about the day: Again professing 1. That I believe that he is in the right that maketh Conscience of the

the Lords day only. 2. But yet I will not break Charity with any Brother that shall in tenderness of Conscience keep both dayes; especially in times of prophaness when few will be brought to the true observation of one. 3. But I think him that keepeth the seventh day only and neglecteth the Lords day, to sin against very evident light, with many aggravations. 4. But I think him that keepeth no day (whether professedly, or practising contrary to his profession; whether on pretence of avoiding Superstition, or on pretence of keeping *every day* as a Sabbath) to be far the worst of all. I shall now add somewhat to some appendant Questions.

CHAP.

CHAP. VIII.

Of the beginning of the Day.

Queſt. 1. **W**Hen doth the Lords day begin?
Anſw. 1. If we can tell when *any day* beginneth, we may know when *that* beginneth. If we *cannot*, the neceſſity of our ignorance, will ſhorten the trouble of our ſcruples by excuſing us.

2. Becauſe the Lords day is not to be kept as a *Jewiſh Sabbath* ceremoniouſly, but the *Time* and the *Reſt* are here commanded ſubſerviently for the *work ſake*, therefore we have not ſo much reaſon to be ſcrupulous about the *hours* of *beginning and ending*, as the Jews had about their Sabbath.

3. I think he that judgeth of the beginning and ending of the day, according to the common eſtimation of the Countrey where he liveth, will beſt anſwer the ends of the Inſtitution. For he will ſtill keep the ſame *proportion* of time; and ſo much as is ordinarily allowed on *other dayes for work*, he will ſpend this day in *holy works*; and ſo much in *reſt* as is uſed to be ſpent in *reſt* on other dayes; (which may ordinarily ſatisfie a well informed Conſcience) And if any extraordinary occaſions (as journeying or the like) require him to doubt of
any

any hours of the night, whether they be part of the Lords day or not, 1. It will be but his *sleeping* time, and not his *worshipping time*, which he will be in doubt of: and 2. He will avoid all *scandal* and *tempting* others to break the day, if he measure the day by the *common estimate*: whereas if the Countrey where he liveth do esteem the day to begin at *Sun-setting*, and he suppose it to begin at *Midnight*, he may be *scandalous* by doing that which in the common opinion is a violation of the day. If I thought that this short kind of solution, were not the fittest to afford just quietness to the minds of sober Christians in this point, I would take the pains to scan the Controversie about the true beginning of dayes: But lest it more puzzle and perplex, than edifie or resolve and quiet the Conscience, I save my self and the Reader that trouble.

CHAP.

CHAP. IX.

Queſt. 2. *How ſhould the Lords day be kept or uſed?*

Anſw. The Practical Directions I have given in another Treatiſe. I ſhall now give you but theſe generals.

I. The day being ſeparated or ſet apart for *Holy Worſhip*, muſt accordingly be ſpent therein. To ſanctifie it, is to ſpend it in holy exerciſes: How elſe ſhould it be uſed as a Holy Day? *I was in the Spirit on the Lords day*, ſaith St. *John*, *Rev.* 1. 10.

II. The principal work of the day is, the *Communion of Chriſtians* in the *publick exerciſes* of Gods worſhip. It is principally to be ſpent in *holy aſſemblies.* And this is the uſe that the Scripture expreſly mentioneth, *Acts* 20. 7. and intimateth 1 *Cor.* 16. 1, 2. And as moſt Expoſitors think, *John* 21. when the Diſciples were gathered together with the door ſhut for fear of the Jews. And all Church Hiſtory aſſureth us, that in theſe *holy Aſſemblies* principally, the day was ſpent by the ancient Chriſtians. They ſpent almoſt all the day together.

3. It is not only to be ſpent in holy exerciſes, but alſo in *ſuch ſpecial* holy exerciſes as are ſuitable to the purpoſes of the day. That is, it
is

is a day of Commemorating the whole work of our *Redemption*; but especially the *Resurrection* of Christ. Therefore it is a day of *Thanksgiving* and *Praise*; and the special services of it must be *Laudatory* and *Joyful* exercises.

4. But yet because it is *sinners* that are called to their work, who are not yet fully delivered from their sin and misery, these *praises* must be mixed with penitent Confessions, and with earnest Petitions, and with diligent Learning the will of God.

More particularly, the publick exercises of the day are 1. Humble and penitent Confessions of sin. 2. The faithful and fervent prayers of the Church. 3. The Reading, Preaching and Hearing of the Word of God. 4. The Communion of the Church in the Lords Supper. 5. The *Laudatory Exhortations* which attend it; And the *singing and speaking of the praises* of our Creator and Redeemer and Sanctifier; with *joyful Thanksgiving* for his wonderful benefits. 6. The seasonable exercise of holy Discipline on particular persons, for comforting the weak, reforming the scandalous, casting out the obstinately impenitent, and absolving and receiving the penitent. 7. The Pastors blessing the people in the name of the Lord. 8. And as an appurtenance in due season, Oblations or Contributions for holy and Charitable uses, even for the Church and Poor, which yet may be put off to other dayes, when it is more convenient so to do.

Qu. *But who is it that must be present in all these exercises?*

Answ.

here there is *no Church* yet called,
y may be spent in *Preaching to*, and
inconverted Infidels: But where there
and *no other persons* mixt, the whole
he day must be such as are fitted to
the *Church*. But where there is
other persons (Infidels, or impeni-
vith them, the day must be spent
ly in exercises suitable to the good
t so that *Church-exercises* should be
work of the day. And the ancient
tice of the Churches was, to *Preach*
l *auditors* and *Catechumens* in the
uch Subjects as were most suitable
then to dismiss them, and retain
or baptized) only; And to *Teach*
Commands of Christ; To *stir them up*
commemoration of Christ and his
and to sing Gods praises, and ce-
ords Supper with Eucharistical ac-
nts and joy. And they never kept
in the Church, without the Lords
which the bare administration of the
t their whole work; but all their
g and Praising exercises, were prin-
used, and connexed to the Lords
ich the Liturgies yet extant do at

w no reason but thus, it should be
east but that this course should be
celebration of the day.
eeing the *Sabbath was instituted in the*
commemorate the work of the Crea-
t be laid by now, because of our commemoration

memoration of the work of our Redemption?

Answ. No: Our Redeemers work is to restore us to the acknowledgement and Love of our Creator. And the Commemoration of our Redemption fitteth us to a holy acknowledgement of the Almighty Creator in his works: These therefore are still to go together; according to their several proper places: Even as the Son is the way to the Father, and we must never separate them in the exercise of our Faith, obedience or Love. A Christian is a sanctified Philosopher: And no man knoweth or acknowledgeth Gods works of Creation and Providence aright, in their true sense, but he that seeth God the Creator and Redeemer, the Beginning, the Governour and the End of all. Other Philosophers are but as those Children, that play with the Book and Letters, but understand not the matter contained in it; or like one that teacheth boyes *nitidè literas pingere, to write a curious hand, while he understands not what he writeth.*

Obj. But to spend so much of the day in publick as you speak of, will tire out the Minister by speaking so long: Few men are able to endure it.

Answ. 1. How did the Christians in the Primitive Churches? They met in the morning, and often (as far as I can gather) parted not till night, (And when they did go home between the Morning and Evening Service, it was but for a little time:)

Obj. Then they made it a fast and not a festival.

Answ. It was not the use then to eat dinners in those hot Countreys; much less three meals a day, as we do now. And they accounted it a

sufficient

:ing, to feast once, at Supper; which
ie first all together at their Church‑
h the Sacrament ; But afterward
convenience of that they feasted at
used only the Sacrament in the
iich change was not made without
e of the Apostles ; *Paul* saying,
Have ye not houses to eat and drink
e ye the Church of God ?
er answer that the work of the day
ccording to the primitive use, it will
re labour to the Minister: Because in
on of the Lords Supper, he is not still
ued speech, but hath the intermission
nd useth shorter Speeches which do
spend him. And the *people* bear a
part, to wit, in Gods praises, which
then in their laudatory tone, and are
by the singing of Psalms (which
: the least part of the work.) And
manner of singing was not like ours,
ind *Tunes melodiously*, (as neither
ebrew, Greek or Latine Poems so
s most think, more like to our Ca‑
ig, or saying; yet it followeth not
ie best way *for us*, seeing use hath
ines and Meeter, and way of singing
r the ends to which we use them,
 the chearful consent of all the
either should any think that it is *a*
rful invention, and a sinful *change*,
ld way of singing (used in Scri‑
and long after) into ours ; For the
singing was not a *Divine institution*,

H but

but a *use*; and several Countreys had their several uses herein: And God commandeth us but to *Praise* him, and *sing Psalmes*, but doth not tell us what *meeter* or *tunes* we shall use, or manner of singing, but leaveth this to the use and convenience of every Countrey: And if our way and tunes be to us by custome more *convenient* than those of other Nations in Scripture times, we have no reason to forsake them, and return to the old (Though yet the old way is not to be judged a thing forbidden.) And we see that custome hath so far prevailed with us, that many thousand Religious people, do cheerfully sing Psalmes in the Church in our Tunes and way, who cannot endure to sing in the Cathedral or the ancient Scripture or primitive way, nor to use so much as the Laudatory Responses.

3. And I further answer that every Church should have more Ministers than one, as the ancient Churches had, besides their Readers; and then one may in speaking ease another.

4. But lastly I answer, that These circumstances being alterable according to the state of Countreys & Conveniences, I do not discommend the custome of our Countrey, and of most Christian Churches in our times, in making an intermission, and going home to dinner; as being fittest to our condition. And then there remaineth the less force in the objection, as to the weariness of the Ministers, or the people.

I forbear to say more of the publick Church-performances, having described them all in a small Book called *Universal Concord*, and having exemplified all except Preaching, in our Reformed

formed Liturgie given in to the Bishops at the *Savoy.*

Only here, I will answer them, who object much that *the Ancient Churches spent not the whole day in exercises of Religion, nor forbad other exercises out of the time of publick worship, because we read of little other observation of it by them, but what was done in the publick Assemblies.*

Answ. 1. We find that they took it to be a sanctified or *separated day* ; And they never distinguish, and say, that *Part of the day only was* separated and sanctified to such uses. If they did, *which part* is the sanctified part of the day ? what houres were they which they thought thus separated ? But there is no such distinction or limitation, in the writings of the ancient Doctors. 2. What need you find much mention, what they did out of the time of publick Worship, when they spent *all the day* frequently at first, and almost all the day in after times (with small intermission) in publick Worship ? Do *you* stay but as long at Church as they did, even almost from Morning till Night, and then you will find little time to Dance or Play in. But yet, 3. There want not Testimonies that they thought it unlawful to spend *any part* of the day, in unnecessary diversions from holy things, as Dr. *Young* hath shewed.

III. So much of the day as can be spared from publick Church-worship,(and diversions of necessity,should be next spent most in *holy family-exercises.* And in those unhappy places where the publick worship is slenderly and negligently performed,(on some small part only of the day) or not at all, or not so as it is lawful to joyne in it, (as in Idolatrous Worship, &c.) there *Family worship* must take up most of the day: And in better places, it must take up so much as the publick Worship spareth.

And here the summ of holy exercises in Families is this (which having elsewhere directed you in, I must but briefly name.)

1. To see that the Family *rise as early* on this day as on others, and make it not a day of *sleep* and *idleness*: And not to suffer them to *violate prophane* or *neglect* the day, by any of the sins hereafter named.

2. To call them together before they go to the solemn Assembly, and to *Pray with them* and *praise God*, and if there be time, to read the Scripture, and tell them what they have to do in publick.

3. To see that Dinner and other common employments make no longer an intermission than is needful; And to advise them that at their *meat* and *necessary business*, they shew by their *holy speeches*, that their minds do not forget the day, and the employments of it.

4. To *sing Gods praises with them*, if there be time, and bring them again together to the Church-assembly.

5. When they return either to take some account of them what they have learned, or to call them together to pray for a blessing on what they have heard, and to sing praises to God, and to urge the things which they have heard upon them.

6. At

6. At Supper to behave themselves soberly and piously: And after Supper to shut up the day in Prayer and Praise; And either then or before, either to examine or exhort inferiours, according as the case of the persons and families shall require (For in some Families it will be best on the same day to take an account of their profiting, and to Catechize them: And in other Families that have leisure, other daies may be more convenient for Catechising and Examinations, that the greater works of the Lords day may not be shortened.)

IV. So much of the day as can be spared from *publick* and *family* worship, must be spent in *secret, holy duties*: such as are, 1. Secret Prayer. 2. Reading of the Scriptures and good Books. 3. Holy Meditation; 4. And the secret Conference of bosome friends. Of which I further adde,

1. That where *publick* or *family worship* cannot be had (as in impious places) there secret duties must be the chief, and make up the defect of others. And it is a great happiness of good Christians who have willing minds, that they have such secret substitutes and supplies; That they have Bibles and so many good Books to read, That they may have a friend to talk with of holy things; But much more that they have a God to go to, and a Heaven to Meditate on, besides so many Sacred Verities.

2. That my judgement is, that in those places where the publick Worship taketh up almost all the day, it is no sin to attend on it to the utmost,

and to omit all such Family and secret exercises as cannot be done, without omission of the publick. And that where the publick exercises allow but a little time at home, the Family duties should take up all that little time, except what some shorter secret Prayers or Meditations may have, which will not hinder family duties. And that it is a sinful disorder to do otherwise. Because the Lords day is principally set apart for *publick worship*; And the more *private or secret* is as it were included in the publick: Your Families are at Church with you; The same Prayers which you would put up in secret, you may (usually) put up in publick, and in Families: And it is a turning Gods Worship into a Ceremony and Superstition, to think that you must necessarily put up the same Prayers in a Closet, which you put up in the Family or Church, when you have not time for both. (Though when you have time, *secret prayer*, hath its proper advantages, which are not to be neglected.) And also, what secret or family duty you have not time for on that day, you may do on another day, when you cannot come to Church Assemblies. And therefore it is an Errour to think that the day must be divided in equal proportions, between *Publick*, *Family*, and *Secret Duties*; Though yet I think it not amiss that some *convenient time* for Family and *Secret* duties be left on that day; but not so much as is spent in publick, nor nothing neer it.

If any shall now object, [*I do not believe that we are bound to all this ado, nor so to tire out our selves in Religious exercises: Where is all this ado commanded us?*] I an-

I answer, 1. I have proved to you that in Nature and in Scripture set together as great a proportion of time as this for holy exercises is required.

2. But O what a Carnal unthankful heart, doth this objection signifie? What, do you account your Love to God, and the Commemoration of his Love in Christ, a *toile*? What if God had only given you *leave*, to lay by your worldly business, and idle talk and Childish play, for one dayes time, and to learn how to be like Christ and Angels, and how to make sure of a Heavenly Glory, should you not gladly have accepted it as an unspeakable benefit? O what hearts have these wretched men that must be constrained by *fear* to all that is good, and holy, and spiritual; and *will have* none of Gods greatest mercies, unless it be for fear of Hell (And they shall never *have them indeed* till they *love them*!) What hearts have those men, that had rather be in an Ale-house, or a Play-house, or asleep, than to be in heart with God? That can find so much pleasure in jesting and idle talking and foolery, that they can better endure it, than to peruse a Map of Heaven, and to read and hear the Sacred Oracles! Who think it a toile to praise their Maker and Redeemer, and a pleasure to game and dance and drink! Who turn the glass upon the Preacher, and grudge if he exceed his hour; and can sit at a Tavern or Alehouse, or hold on in any thing thats vain, many hours and never complain of weariness! Do they not tell the world what enemies they are to God, who love a pair of Cards, or Dice, or Wanton Dalliance,

better than his Word and Worship ? Who think six dayes together little enough for their worldly work and profit, and one day in seven too much to spend in the thoughts of God and life Eternal ? Who love the dung of this present World, so much better than all the joyes above, as that they are weary to hear of Heaven above an hour at a time, and long to be wallowing in the dirt again ? Is it not made by the Holy Ghost, a mark not only of *wicked* men, but of men *notoriously wicked*, to be *Lovers of pleasures more than of God ?* 2 Tim. 3. 4.

O Sinners, that in these workings of the wickedness and malignity of your hearts, you would at last but know your selves ! Is it not the *Carnal mind that is thus at enmity to God, and neither is nor can be subject to his Law,* Rom. 8. 6, 7, 8 ? Which will you take to be your friend ; Him that *loveth your* company ; or him that is a weary of it, and is glad when he hath done with you, and is got away ? What would you think of Wife, or Child, or Friend, if they should reason as you do, and say, *What Law doth bind me to be so many hours in the House, or Company, or Service* of my Husband, my Father, or my Friend ? You do not use if you have a Feast, or a Cup of Wine before you, to ask, *Where doth God Command me to Eat or Drink it ?* You can do this without a *Command* ! If you hear but of a *gainful Market* ; you ask not, Where doth God make it my duty to go to it ? If one would give you *Money* or *Land,* you would scarcely ask, How prove you that I am bound to take it ? You would be glad of Leave, without
Commands,

Commands. If the King should say to you, Ask what you will, and I will give it you, you would not say, Where am I bound of God to ask? And when God saith, Ask and it shall be given you, you say, How prove you that I am bound to ask? You can sing ribble songs, and Dance without a Command; You can Feast, and Play, and Prate, and Sleep, and Loyter in Idleness without a Command; But you cannot learn how to be saved, nor praise your Redeemer without a Command. A Thief can Steal, a Fornicator can Play the Bruit, a Drunkard can be Drunk, an Oppressour can make himself hateful to the Oppressed, not only without Law, but against it? But you cannot Rejoice in God, nor live one day together in his Love and Service, without a Law, no nor *with* it neither. For because you had rather not Love him, it is certain that you *do not* Love him: And because you had rather play than pray, and serve the flesh than serve your Maker; it is a certain sign that you *do not* serve him, with any thing which he will accept as Service. For while he hath not your hearts, he hath nothing which he accepteth. Your Knee and Tongue only is forced against your will to that which you call serving him: But your Hearts or Wills cannot be forced. When you had rather be elsewhere, and say When will the Sermon and Prayer be done, that I may be at my Work or Play? God taketh it as if you were there where you had rather be.

I pray you deal openly, and tell me, you that think a day too long for God, and are

weary

weary of all holy work, What would you be doing that while, if you had your choice? Is it any thing which you dare say *is better*? Dare you say that *playing* is better than Praying, and Dancing is better than praising God with Psalms? Or that your Sleep, or Games, or Chat or Worldly business is better than the Contemplation of God and Glory! And will those deceivers of the people also say this, who teach them that it is a tedious uncommanded thing, to serve God so long? I think they dare not speak it out. If they dare, let them not grudge that they must be for ever shut out of Heaven, where there will be nothing else but holiness. But if you dare not say so, Why will you choose the worse before the better? Why will you be weary of well doing, that you may do ill? Why are you not more weary of every thing than of holiness, unless you think every thing better than holiness.

Especially those men, 1. Whose *judgement* is for *will-worship*, should not ask, where is there a Command for any good which they are willing of. But doth not this shew that you had rather there were *no Command* for it? Be judges your selves. 2. And they that are for making the Churches a great deal more work than God hath made them, (O what abundance hath Popery made, and what a multitude of new Religious particles!) methinks should not for shame say that God hath tired them out, and made them too much work already? Do you cry out, What a weariness is this one day, when you
would

would adde of your own such a multitude of more dayes, and more work?

Yet though I talk of doing it willingly if you had no *forcing Law* of God, but *bare leave* to receive such Benefits, my meaning is not that God hath left any *such things indifferent* or made them only the matter of *Counsels* and not of *Commands*: For he hath made it our *duty* to receive our *own benefits,* and to do that which tendeth to our *own good* and Salvation. But if it *had been so,* that we had only leave to receive so great mercies without any other penalty for refusing, than the *loss* of them, it should be enough to men that Love themselves, and know what is for their good. Much more when commands concurr.

CHAP.

CHAP. X.

How the Lords day should not be spent: Or, What is unlawful on it?

AS to the resolving of this Question also, I would wish for no greater advantage on him that I dispute with, but that he be a man that *Loveth God and Holiness*, and knoweth somewhat of the difference between things temporal and things Eternal; and knoweth what is for the good of his soul; and preferreth it before his body; and hath an appetite to relish the delights of Wisdom, and of things most excellent and Divine. And that he be one that knoweth his own necessities, and repenteth of his former loss of time; and liveth in a daily preparation for death; that is, that he be a real Christian; And then by all this it will appear, how the *Lords day must not be spent*; or what things are *unlawful to be done thereon*.

1. Undoubtedly it must not be spent in *wickedness*: In *gluttony or drunkenness, chambering or wantonness, strife or envying,* or any of those works of the flesh, which are *at all times* sinful. An evil work is most unsuitable to a *holy day*. And yet, alas, what day hath more ryotting ring and excess, of meat, and drink, and wantonness, and sloth, and lust, than it?

II. It ought not to be spent in our worldly businesses, which are the labours allowed us on the six dayes; unless *Necessity* or *Mercy* make them at any time become such duties of the Law of Nature, as Positives must for that time give place to. For how is it a day separated to holy employments, if we spend it in the common business of the world? It is the great advantage that we have by such a separated day, that we may wholly call off our minds from the world, and set them on the world to come, and exercise them in holy communion with God and his Church, without the interruptions and distractions of any earthly cogitations. A divided mind doth never perform any holy work, with that integrity and life, as the nature of it requireth. Heavenly contemplations are never well managed with the intermixture of diverting worldly thoughts: So great a work as to converse in Heaven, to be rapt up in the admirations of the Divine perfections, to kindle a fervent Love to God, by the contemplation of his Love and Goodness, to triumph over sin and Satan with our triumphing glorified Head, to Commemorate his Resurrection, and the whole work of our Redemption with a lively working faith, doth require the whole heart, and will not consist with aliene thoughts, and the diversion of fleshly employments or delights. Nay, had we no higher work to do, than to search our hearts, and lament our sins, and beg

for

for mercy, and learn Gods Word, and treat with our Redeemer about the saving of our souls, and to prepare for death and judgement, surely it should challenge all our faculties, and tell us that voluntary diversions, do too much favour of impiety and contempt. It is the great mercy of God, that we have leave to lay by these clogs and impediments of the soul, and to seek his face with greater freedom, than the incumbrances of our week day labours will allow us. No slave can be so glad of a Sabbaths ease from his sorest toil and basest drudgery, as a believer should be to be released from his earthly thoughts and business, that he may freely, entirely and delightfully converse with God.

III. The Lords day must not be spent in tempting, diverting, unnecessary recreations, or pleasures of the flesh. 1. For these are as great an impediment to the holy employment of the soul, as worldly labours, if not much more. It is easier for a man to be exercised in heavenly cogitations, at the Plow or Cart, or other such labours of his place and Calling, than at Bowls, or Hunting, or Cards, or Dice, or Stage-playes, or Races, or Dancing, or Bear-baitings, or Cock-fights, or any such sensual sports. I need no proof of this to any man, that hath himself any experience, of the holy employments of a believing soul, or that ever knew what it was to spend one Day of the Lord aright; And no proof will suffice them that have

because they know not effectually they talk of.

that even on other daies, the worst addicted to these sports, and are eaders for them, and that the more the worse they grow; yea that the them are frequently the times of of many heynous sins. I have lived in many places where sometimes couth Spectacles have been their ain seasons of the year, and some-:e-dancings, and sometimes Stage-)metimes *Wakes* and *Revels*; And ved that these were the times of the s crimes; and that there was then nness, more fighting, more horrid .irses uttered than in many weeks at Then it was that the enraged sen-.ct the part of furious Devils, in reviling all that were soberer and .emselves, and railing at those that and their everlasting state, as Preci-s and Hypocrites; Then it was that dy in their fury, if they durst, to ry persons and houses of them that) as they did. Whatever is done des and Tumults, is done with the »f rage and passion, and with the city, and the violation of all Laws ng restraints. As many waters ous stream, and great fires where conjunct do disdain restraint, and ur all before them; so is it with the)f Youth, when voluptuous persons
once

once get together, and their lusts take fire, and they fall into a torrent of profuse sensuality. Yea those that at other times are sober, and when they come home do seem of another mind, yet do as the rest when they are among them, and seem as bad and furious as they: As we see among the *London* Apprentices on the day called *Good-tides Tuesday*, or *May day*, when they once get out together and are in motion, they seem all alike, and those that are most sober and timerous alone, in the rowt are heightened to the audacity of the rest; And as in an Army the sight of the multitude, and the noise of Drums and Guns, puts valour into the fearful; and they will go on with others, that else would run away from a proportionable single combate and danger; And as Boyes at School that fear to offend singly, yet fear not to barr out their Master in a combination when all concurr; so all seem wicked in a crowd and rowt of wicked persons; And sensuality and licentiousness is not the smallest part of wickedness.

O how unfit is Youth in such a Crowd, to think of God, or Eternity, or Death; or to hear the sober warnings of a Preacher, in comparison of what the same persons be, when they are at Church, and Congregated purposely to hear Gods Word. Go among them and try them then, with any grave and wholesome Counsel: Ask them whether they are penitent Converts, and whether they are prepared for another world. Try what answer they will give you, and whether they will not deride you more than at another time? I would those that write and plead

for

for this under the name of *harmleß recreations*, would go amongst them sometimes with sober Counsel, and learn to be wise by their own experience; that their errours might not be of such pernicious consequence to mens souls as it hath been. Reason it self hath no place or audience in the noise of youthful furious lusts. They will laugh at *Reason*, as well as at *Scripture*; and scorn *sobriety*, as well (though not so much) as *holineß*. If even in the meetings of grave persons, it have ever been observed that individual persons are apt to be carryed by the stream, and otherwise than their talk importeth at other times when they are single, what wonder if it be so in evil with unbridled youth?

If you say that the *Law forbiddeth rowts and riots, and it is no such unruly assemblies that we defend.*

Answ. Disclaim not the *name* only while you defend the thing. Be not like them that say, We perswade men to *voluntary untruths* but not to *lying*; to *break their Vows and Oathes in lawful matters*, but not to perjury; to kill those that anger them, but not to murder; to take other mens goods by force, but not to robbery, &c. Is not a *Wakes* and *Revels* and *Morrice-Dances*, and Dancing-assemblies, and Spectacles, and Stage plays, and the like, such a concourse as I am speaking of. Do you limit Dancers, and Players to any numbers? I speak not of the Laws. I am too much unacquainted with them. If they say, that above *four meeting* to Dance or Drink on the Lords day shall be accounted a Conventicle or unlawful Assembly,

I it

it is more than ever I heard of; But I am speaking of the common practice of the contrary, and of those that ordinarily defend it, and labour to bring both Godly Ministers, and sober people, under the scorn of foolish precisenefs and superstition, because they would hinder the sin and ruine of the people. If you will allow them to assemble for their Dancings, *Shews*, and Sports, you will encourage them to break the Laws both of God and Man, though you pretend never so much care that they be observed. You may as well allow them to be Drunk, and when you have done, forbid them to break Gods Laws and the Kings in their Drunkenness. There are few in such sportful Assemblies that are not Drunk with Concupiscence, and whose reason is not drowned in voluptuousness and vain imaginations. Let those Divines (if I may so call the Advocates of Sensuality and Sin) which are otherwise minded, give us leave to oppose against all their Cavils, and the false names of *harmless recreations*, but, 1. Our own experience, who in our youth, have alwaies found such sports and revelling Assemblies to be corrupters of our minds, and temptations to evil, and quenchers of every holy motion, and enemies to all thats good. 2. The experience of the visibly corrupted undone sensual youth, that are round about us, in all Countreys where we have lived. 3. And the judgement of *Solomon*, (who saith as much for pleasure as any Sacred Writer.) Eccl. 7. 2, 3, 4, 5, 6. *It is better to go to the house of mourning, than to the house of feasting: For that is the end of all men, and the living will lay it to his heart: Sorrow is*

better

better than laughter; for by the sadness of the Countenance the heart is made better. The heart of the wise is in the house of mourning, but the heart of fools is in the house of mirth. (I pray you do not say I raile at you by the reciting of these words, nor that I diminish the honour of the Reverend Advocates for *Wakes* and Lords day Sports and Dancings:) It is better to hear the rebuke of the wise, than for a man to hear the Song of fools. For as the sound of thorns under a pot, so is the laughter of the fool.]

3. Moreover, these sports, and pleasures, and riotings, are worse than Plowing and Labouring on the Lords day, because (as they are more adverse to spiritual and heavenly joyes, so) they do *less good* to recompense the hurt. A *Carpenter*, a *Mason*, a *Plowman*, &c. may do *some good* by his unlawful, unseasonable labour; some one may be the better for it: But, Dancing, and Sports, and Gaming, do no good but hurt. They corrupt the Fantasie; They imprint upon the *Thinking faculty*, so strong an inclination to run out after such things; and upon the Appetite so strong a lift and longing for them, that carnality is much encreased by them; Mortification hindred; Concupiscence gratified; the flesh prevaileth, the spirit is quenched; and the soul made as unfit for heavenly things, as a School-boy is for his Book, whose heart is set upon his play: Yea abundance more; as Nature by Corruption is more averse to spiritual things, than to the things of Art or Nature.

4. These Dancings, and Playes, and Wakes and other riotous sports, are a strong temptation also

also to them that are not of the riotous societies, but have convictions on their hearts, that they have greater and better things to mind. Without accusing others, I may say that I know this by bad experience. I cannot forget, when my Conscience was against their courses, and called me to better things, how hardly when I was young, I passed by the Dancing, and the Playing Congregations; and especially when in the Passage I must bear their scorn.

And I was one Year a School-master, and found how hard it was for the poor Children, to avoid such snares, even when they were sure to be whipt the next day for their pleasures.

5. And those Riots and Playes are injurious to the pious and sober persons who dislike them. For it is *they* that shall be made the Rabbles Scorn, and the Drunkards Song; Besides that the noise oft times annoyeth them when they should be calmely serving God. And they are hindered from governing and instructing their Families, while their Children and Servants are thus tempted to be gone, and their hearts are all the while in the playing place. Never did a hungry dog more grudge at his restraint from meat, than Children and young Servants usually grudge, to be Catechised, or kept to holy exercises, when they hear the pipe, or the noise of the licentious multitude in the Streets. I cannot forget, that in my Youth in those late times, when we lost the labours of some of our Conformable Godly Teachers, for not Reading publickly the Book for Sports and Dancing on the

Lords

Lords dayes, one of my Fathers own Tenants was the Town Piper, hired by the Year (for many Years together) and the place of the Dancing Assembly was not an hundred yards from our door; and we could not on the Lords day, either read a Chapter, or Pray, or sing a Psalm, or Catechise or instruct a Servant, but with the noise of the Pipe and Taber, and the Whootings in the Street, continually in our Ears; And even among a tractable people, we were the common Scorn of all the Rabble in the Streets, and called Puritans, Precisians and Hypocrites, because we rather chose but to read the Scriptures, than to do as they did (Though there was no favour of any Non-conformity in our Family.) And when the people by the Book were allowed to Play and Dance, out of publick *Service-time*, they could so hardly break off their Sports, that many a time the Reader was fain to stay till the Piper and Players would give over; And sometimes the Morrice-Dancers would come into the Church, in all their Linnen and Scarfs and Antick Dresses, with Morrice-bells jingling at their leggs. And as soon as Common Prayer was read, did haste out presently to their Play again. Was this a Heavenly Coversation? Was this a help to holiness and Devotion? or to the Mortification of fleshly Lusts? Was this the way to train up youth in the Nurture and Admonition of the Lord? And were such Assemblies like to the primitive Churches? Or such Families governed Christianly and in the fear of God? O Lord set wise and holy Pastors over thy poor flocks, that have learnt themselves the holy

I 3   Doctrine

Doctrine which they Preach, and who love, (or at least abhorr not) the service and imitation of a Crucified Christ, and the practice of that Religion which they themselves profess.

Obj. But poor labouring people must have some recreation, and they cannot through their poverty have leisure any other day.

Ansr. 1. A sad Argument to be used by them, that by racking of Rents do keep them in Poverty. They that cannot live without all those superfluities, which requireth many hundred pounds a Year to maintain them, must for this gratifying pride and fleshly lusts, set such bargains to their poor Tenants, as that they confess they cannot live, without taking the Lords day to recreate them from the toile and weariness of their excessive labours: And will not God judge such self-condemning oppressours as these are?

2. But is this an Argument fit for the mouth of a Minister or any Christian, who knoweth how much the soul is more worth than the body? and Eternity more valuable than the pleasures of this little time? If Poverty deny the people liberty to play on the week dayes, doth it not as much deny them liberty to Pray, and to read the Scriptures, and to learn their Catechisms, and the Word of God? Surely it better beseemeth any man that believeth another life, a Heaven and a Hell, to say, Poor Labourers have so little time, to Learn, to Meditate, to Read, to Pray, on the Week dayes, that if they do not follow it close upon the Lords day, they are like to perish in their ignorance: (For if the Gospel be hid, it is hid to them that are lost, 2 *Cor.* 4. 3.) which do you

you think it better to leave undone, if one of them must be left undone? Whether the learning of Gods Word, or the Pleasures and Recreations of the flesh?

3. It is either their *Bodies* or their *Minds*, that need Recreation. When the Body is tired with toilesome labour, it is *ease*, rather than toilesome Dancings or Plays, that are fit to recreate it. Or else God will be charged with mistake in the reasons of the ancient Sabbath. But if it be the *Mind* that needeth *recreation*, why should not the Learning of Heavenly truth, and the Joyful Commemoration of our Redemption, and the foresight of Heaven and the Praises of God, be more delightful than the noise of Thornes under a pott; even than the laughter and sport of fools, or than the Dancings and Games that now you plead for? But the truth is, It is not the Minds of poor labouring men, that are over-workt and tired on the week dayes; but it is their *bodies*: And therefore there is no Recreation so suitable to them, as the ease of the body, and the holy and joyful exercise of the mind, upon their Creator, their Redeemer, and their Everlasting Rest.

4. But if you will needs have daies of temptation and sinful sports and pleasures for them, let Landlords abate their Tenants as much Rent, as one dayes vacancy from labour in a Month or a Fortnight will amount to; or let the Common Saints dayes, which of the two are more at mans disposal, be made their sporting dayes, and rob not their souls of that one weekly day, which God hath separated for his Worship.

Obj.

Obj. But there are *Students, and Lawyers, and Ministers, and Gentlemen, whose labour is most that of the Brain, and not the Plow-mans bodily toile; and these have need of bodily Recreation.*

Answ. And there are few of these so poor but they can take their bodily Recreation on the week dayes: And many of them need as much the whole Lords day for their souls Edification as any others: And no one that knoweth himself will say that he needs it not. If any men need remission of Studies, and bodily Exercise it is Ministers themselves: And is it themselves that they plead for Sports and Dancing for? Would they be companions of the vain in such like vanities?

Obj. But *the mind of man is not able to endure a constant intension and elevation of devotion all the day long without recreation and intermission; And putting men upon more than they can do, will but hinder them; when a little recreation will make them more fresh and fervent when they return to God.*

Answ. O what an advantage is it to know by experience what one talketh of? And what an inconvenience to talk of Holiness and Heavenliness by hearsay only! 1. To poor people that have but one day in seven, that one day should not seem too long. 2. If it be from a Carnal enmity to God and spiritual things, shortness and seldomness will be no Cure. But they have need rather to be provoked to diligence till they are cured, than to be indulged in that averseness and sloth, which till its cured will prevail, when you have done your best against it. 3. But if it be a weariness of the flesh, as the Disciples when they

they slept while Christ was Praying, or a weariness through such imperfection of Grace and Remnant of Carnality, which the sincere are lyable to, then giving way to it will increase it, and resisting it is the way to overcome it. 4. How many necessary intermissions are there, which confute this pretense of *weariness?* Some time is taken up in dressing; And some with poor Servants in waiting on their Masters and Mistrisses, and in preparing Meat and drink; some in going to Church and coming home; some in eating, usually more than once; some in preparing again for sleep; besides what Cattle and by-occasions will require? And is the remainder of *one day* in a week yet too much for the business which we are Created, preserved, and Redeemed for, and on which our endless life dependeth? O that we knew what the Love of God is? and what it is to regard our souls according to their worth! Would not a soul that loveth God rather say, *Alas, how short is the Lords day? How quickly is it gone? How many interruptions hinder my delight?* Shall I think a Week short enough for my worldly labours,) and one day (thus parcelled) too long to seek the face of God? I see blind Worldlings and sensualists can be longer unwearied at Market, in their Shops and Fields, especially when their gain comes in; and at Cards and Dice, and Bowling and idle Prating, *&c.* And shall I be weary so soon of the most noble and necessary Work, and of the sweetest pleasures upon Earth?

An Hypocrite that draweth near to God but with the lips, whilest his heart is far from him, as
he

he never truly seeketh God, so he never truly findeth him, and hath none of the true spiritual delights of holiness, nor ever feeleth the pleasure of exercising his *Love to God* by the help of *faith*, in the *hopes* of *Heaven*: And therefore no wonder if he be weary of such unprofitable, sapless and unpleasant work, as his dead formalities and affectations are. But it is not so with the sincere experienced Christian, who serving God in *spirit* and *truth*, hath *true* and *spiritual* recreation, pleasure and benefit in and by his Service. And therefore we see that the holy experienced believers, are still averse to these sensual diversions; and do not think the Lords day or his Service too long. And O Christian what a happy advantage in such controversies have you, in your holy sincerity and sweet experience?

5. But yet I am not such a stranger to man, to my self or others, as to deny that our naughty hearts are inclined to be weary of well doing: But mark what a cure God in Wisdom and mercy hath provided for us: As it is but one day in seven which is thus to be wholly employed with God, and as much of this day is taken up with the bodily necessaries aforesaid; so for the rest, God appointeth us variety of exercises, that when we are weary of one, another may be our recreation. When we have *heard* we must *pray*, and when we have *prayed* we must *hear* again: We must Read, we must Sing and speak Gods Praises, we must celebrate the memorial of Christs death in the Sacrament; we must Meditate; we must Conferr, we must instruct our Families: And we have variety of
subjects

subjects for each of these. As a student that is weary hath variety of Books and Studies to recreate his mind; so hath every Christian variety of holy employment on the Lords day. And all of it excellent profitable and delightful! Christian, believe not that Minister or Man whatever he be, that telleth thee that Chrisis Yoak is heavy, or that his Commandments are grievous. Hath he done so much to deliver us from the strait Yoak, the heavy Burden, and the grievous Commandments? and now shall we accuse him of bringing us under a toylesome task? Is it a toile to love or count your money? to love and look upon your Corn and Cattle? to love and converse with your Friend? to feast your Body on the pleasantest Food? If not, why should it be a toile to any but a wicked heart, to spend a day in Loving God, and hearing the Messages of his Love to us, and in the foresight and foretasts of everlasting love.

Caviller, come but unto Christ, and cast off the wearisome, toilesome burden of thy sin, and Satans drudgery, and take Christs Yoak and Burden on thee; and learn of him, and try then whether his daies and work be grievous. Come and spend but a day in *Loving God*, as thou dost in *talking* of him, and try whether Love, and the holiest Love, be a wearisome work. But if thou wilt make a Religion of all Shell and no Kernel, all Carkass and no Life, like that which the *Jansenists* charge the Jesuites with, that say, *We are bound to love God but once in four or five years, or once in all our lives*, no wonder if thou be weary of such a *Religion*.

6. But

6. But I will tell them that are the Teachers of the people, an honester way to Cure the peoples weariness, than to send them to a Piper or to a Play to cure it. Preach with such life and awakening seriousness; Preach with such grateful holy eloquence, and with such easie method, and with such variety of wholesome matter, that the people may never be aweary of you. Pour out the rehearsal of the Love and benefits of God, open so to them the priviledges of faith, and the Joyes of hope, that they may never be aweary. How oft have I heard the people say of such as these, *I could hear him all day and never be aweary!* They are troubled at the shortness of such Sermons and wish they had been longer. Pray with that Heavenly life and fervour as may rap up the souls of those that joyne with you, and try then whether they will be aweary: Praise God with that joyful alacrity which beseemeth one that is ready to pass into Glory, and try whether this will not Cure the peoples weariness.

Misunderstand me not. I am now speaking to none but guilty hypocrites, and not to any faithful holy Ministers; And to such I say, when you have done nothing but coldly read over the publick Prayers, or as coldly and crudely added your own, and tired the hearers, with a dry, a sapless, lifeless, unexperienced discourse, and then send them as a wearied people, to dancing and sports for a needful recreation, is this like the work of a Pastour of Souls. When you have cryed down *other mens* Praying and Preaching, and then tell the people that the *Praying* and *Preaching* which you recommend to them as

better,

better, will not digest well, without a Dance or Recreation after it, to expel the peoples weariness; is not this to disgrace your own Prayers and Preaching which you before commended to them? And when you have done, if after this you speak against others for their long Praying, and for so much Preaching and Hearing, as if they never had enough, is not this to *commend* what you *discommend*? and to tell the people that those mens Praying and Preaching whom you revile, is such as doth *not weary their* Auditours; when *yours* is such, as will tire men, if it be long, or if they be not Recreated after it with a Piper, a Fidler, or a Dance? O that the *Ithacian* Bishops of the World, and all the Clergie of their mind, would at least hear *Hooker* in the Preface to his *Eccles. pol.* how little their cause is beholden to such Patrons, and how well it might spare them!

For my own part, as my flesh is weak, so my heart is too bad, too backward to these Divine and Heavenly works! And yet I never have time to spare. God knoweth that it is my daily groans, *How great is work, yea and how sweet; and how short is the day, the week, the year! How quickly is it night! How fast do weeks and years roll away!* And shall any man that is called a Minister of Christ, perswade poor *Labourers* and *Servants* who have but one day for retirement from the world, to converse with God without distraction, that *this one day is too long*, and that their work must be eased by carnal sports? Nay shall a man that would be called a Minister or a Christian, perswade men against all the experience
of

of the World, that the diversions and interruptions of a *Dance* or *May game*, or a Race or a Comedie, will dispose their minds to return to God with more Heavenly alacrity and purity than before, or than variety of holy exercises will do? Or rather, are we constrained to say (though it displease) that Hypocrites are all for Imagery and hypocritical Religion; and that whether he be at Church or at home, in Praying or in drinking and sensuality and voluptuosness, a Worldling is every where a Worldling still, and an hypocrite is an hypocrite still; And it is not his Book or Pulpit that maketh him another man. And that as the man is, such will be his Work. *Operari sequitur esse.* And that the Jesuites are not the only men in the world, that would make a Religion to suite mens lusts, and would serve Satan and the flesh, in the livery of Christ. But I fear I have been too long on this objection.

IV. The *Lords day* must not be spent in *Idleness*: not in unnecessary sleep, or in vain walking, or vain talking, or long dressings, or too long feastings, or any thing unnecessary which diverteth our souls from their Sacred seasonable work. It is not a Jewish Ceremonious Sabbath of bodily rest which we are to keep: But it is a day of holy and spiritual works: of the needfullest work in all the world: To do that which is ten thousand times more necessary and excellent, than all our labours and provision for the flesh. And if no man hath time to spare on the week day, but he that knoweth not aright what it is to be a Christian or a man

man or why God maintaineth and continueth him in the world; What shall we think of them that can find time to spare on the Lords own day, and can walk and idle away the most precious of all their time? If it be folly to cast away your Silver, it is not wisdom to cast away your gold. O that God would but open mens eyes, to see what is before them, and how near to Eternity they stand, and awaken mens sleepy sensual souls, to live as men that do not *dream* of another world, but unfeignedly believe it; and then a little reasoning would serve turn to convince them, that the Lords day should be spent in the duties of serious holiness, and not in Idleness, or unnecessary works or sports.

Obj. *But by all this you seem to cast a great reproach on* Calvin, Beza, *and most of the great Divines of the forreign Churches, who have not been so strict for the observation of the Lords day.*

Answ. Let these things be observed by the impartial Reader. 1. It cannot be proved to be most of them, that were so faulty herein as the objection intimateth. Many of them have written much for the holy spending of the day. 2. It must be noted, that it is a superstitious Ceremonious Sabbatizing which many of them write against, who seem to the unobservant to mean more. It is not the spending of the day in spiritual exercises. 3. And you must remember that they came newly out of Popery, and had seen the Lords day and a superabundance of other Humane Holy dayes imposed on the Churches to be Ceremoniously observed, and they did not all

of

of them so clearly as they ought, discern the difference between the Lords day and those holy dayes or Church Festivals, and so did too promiscuously conjoine them in their reproofs of the burdens imposed on the Church. And it being the Papists Ceremoniousness, and their multitude of Festivals that stood all together in their eye, it tempted them to too undistinguishing and unaccurate a reformation. 4. And for *Calvin* you must know that he spent every day so like to a Lords day, in hard Study, and Prayer, and numerous Writings, and publick Preaching, or Lecturing and Disputings, either every day in the week, or very near it, scarce allowing himself time for his one only spare meale a day, that he might the easilier be tempted, to make less difference in his judgement between the Lords day and other dayes, than he should have done, and to plead for more recreation on that day for others, than he took on any day himself. 5. And then his followers having also many of the same temptations, were apt to tread in his steps through the deserved estimation of his worth and judgement and lest they should seem to be of different minds. But as *England* hath been the happyest in this piece of reformation, so all men are unexcusable that will encourage idleness, sensuality or neglect of ● important duties of the day.

CHAP.

CHAP. XI.

What things should not be Scrupled as unlawful on the Lords day.

AS I have told you the Lords day is not a Sabbath in the Jewish sense, or a day of *Ceremonious Rest*, but a Day of Worshiping our Creator and Redeemer with thankful Commemorations and with holy Joy, *&c.* And a day of vacancy from such earthly things as may be any hinderance to this holy work; so now I must resolve the Question first in the *General*, that nothing lawful at another time is unlawful on this day, which hath not the *Nature* of an Impediment to *the holy duties* of the day; unless it be accidentally on the account of *scandal* or ill example unto others, or disobeying the Laws of Magistrates, or crossing the Concord of the Churches, or such like. Therefore hence I deduce these particular resolutions following.

I. It is not unlawful to be at such *bodily* or *mental* labour as is needful to the spiritual duties of the day. If the *Priests in the Temple* (saith Christ) *did break the Sabbath and were blameless* (that is, not the Command of God to them for keeping the Sabbath, but the external Rest of the

K   Sabbath,

Sabbath, which was commanded to others with an exception to their case,) we may well say that it is no sin, for a Minister now to spend *his strength* in laborious Preaching and Praying; or for the people to travel as far as is needful, to the Church Assemblies: nor do we need to tye our selves to a Sabbath dayes journey, (that is, according to the Scribes 2000 Cubits, which is 3000 feet, and *quinque stadia*:) It is lawful to go many miles when it is necessary to the work of the day.

II. It is not unlawful to be at the labour of dressing our selves somewhat more ornately or comely than on another day. Because it is suitable to the rejoycing of a Festival. But to waste time needlesly in curiosity, and proud attiring, to the hinderance of greater things, is detestable.

III. It is not unlawful to dress meat, even in some fuller and better manner than on other dayes; Because it is a Festival, or day of Thanksgiving. And it is a vain self-contradiction of some men, who think that another day of Thanksgiving is not well kept, if there be not two feasting meals at least, and yet think it unlawful to dress one on the Lords day: But yet to make it a day of Gluttony, or to waste more of the day in eating or dressing meat than is agreeable to the spiritual work of the day, which is our end; or to make our selves sleepy by fulness; or to use our servants like Beasts, to provide for our bellies, with the neglect of their

own

own souls; or to pamper the flesh to the satisfaction and irritation of its lusts; All this is to be detested.

IV. It is not unlawful to do the necessary works of mercy to our selves or others, to man or beast; *Those which must be done, and cannot be delayed without more hurt than the doing of them will procure* (for that is the description of a necessary work.) As to eat and drink and cloth our selves, and our Children; To carry meat to the poor that are in present necessity; To give or take Physick; and to go for advice to the Physician or Surgeon: To travel upon a business of importance and necessity; To quench a fire; or prop a house that is about to fall; To march or fight in a necessary case of Warr; To Saile or labour at Sea in cases of necessity; To Boat men over a River that go to Church; To pursue a Robber, or defend him that is assaulted; To pull a man out of fire or water; To dress a mans sores, or to give Physick to the sick; To pull an Oxe or Horse or other Cattle out of a pit or water; To drive or lead them to water, and to give them meat: To save Cattle, Corne or Hay from the sudden inundations of the Sea, or of Rivers, or from Floods; To drive Cattle or Swine out of the grounds where they break in to spoile; such necessary actions are not unlawful but a duty; It being a Moral or Natural precept, which Christ twice bid the Ceremonious Pharises learn [*I will have mercy and not Sacrifice.*]

And it is not only works of neceffity to a *mans life*, that are here meant by *neceffary works*; But fuch alfo as are *neceffary to* a fmaller and lower end or ufe.

And yet it is not *all fuch neceffity* neither that will allow us to do the thing. Otherwife a Tradefman or Plowman might fay that his labour is neceffary to the *getting* or *faving* of this or that fmall commodity; I fhall be a lofer if I do not Work. And on the other fide, if it were only a neceffity for life, limbs or livelihood that would allow us labour, than it would be unlawful to drefs Meat, and to drive Cattle out of the Corn, and many fuch things before mentioned; And then it would be lawful to give meat only to Oxen or Horfes of great price, and not to Hens, Ducks, Geefe, Dogs, and other Animals of little value.

Therefore there is a great deal of prudent difcretion neceffary to the avoiding of extreams. God hath not enumerated all the particulars which are allowed or forbidden in their generals. What then fhall we do? Shall we violate the outward reft of the day for the worth of a Groat or two Pence (as the feeding of Hens or fuch like may be?) Or fhall we fuffer the lofs of many pounds rather than ftirr to fave them? As for inftance, Is it lawful to open, or turn, or carry in Corn or Hay, which in all rational probability (though not certainly) is like to be loft or very much fpoiled, if it be let alone to the next day? The Corn or Hay may be of many pounds value, when the feeding of Swine or Hens may be little: The Corn or Hay is like to be be lost; when the Swine, or Hens, or Horses, or Oxen, may easily recover the hunger or abstinence of a day? What must be done in such cases as these?

I answer, 1. It is necessary to know that where God hath not made particular determinations, yet general Laws do still oblige us.

2. And that Christian Prudence is necessary to the right discerning how far our actions fall under those General Laws of God.

3. That he that will discern these things must be a man, that truly understandeth, valueth and loveth the true Ends and Work of the Lords day, and not a man that hateth it, or careth not for it; And a man that hath a right estimate also of those outward things, which stand in question to be medled with. And he must be one that hath no superstitious Jewish conceits of the external Rest of the day: And he must be one that looketh, not only to one thing or a few, but to *all things* how numerous soever which the determination of his case dependeth on.

4. And because very few are such, it is needful that those few that are such, be Casuists and Advisers to the rest, and that the more ignorant consult with them (especially if they be their proper Pastors) as they do with Physicians and Lawyers for their health and their estates.

5. It must be known that oft times the Laws of the Land do interpose in such cases; And if they do determine so strictly, as to forbid that which else would to some be lawful, they must be obeyed; Because bad men cannot be kept from doing ill by excesses, unless some good men be hindered by the same Laws from some things

that are to them indifferent, nay possibly eligible, if there were no such Law.

6. And accordingly the case of *Scandal* or *Temptation* to others, that will turn our Example to their sin, must be considered in our Practice. Yea it is not only things meerly Indifferent that we must deny our liberty in, to prevent anothers fall, but oft times that which would else be a *Duty* may become a sin, when it will scandalize another, or tempt him to a farr greater and more dangerous sin. As it may be my duty to speak some word, or do some action, as most useful and beneficial, when there is nothing against it; And yet if I may foresee that another will turn that speech or action to his ruine, to the hatred of piety, or to take occasion from it to exercise cruelty upon other Christians, &c. it may become my hainous sin. So it must here be considered, who will know of the Action which you do? and what use they are like to make of it?

7. And a little publick hurt must be more regarded than more private benefit; And the hurt of a mans soul cannot be countervailed by your corporal Commodities.

8. These things being premised, I suppose that the great Rule to guide you in such undetermined Circumstances is the *Interest* of *the End*; All things must be done to the Glory of God, and to Edification. A truly impartial prudent man can discern by comparing all the circumstances whether his action (as if it were carrying in Endangered Corn) were likely to do more good or harm? On one side you must put in the ballance the value of the thing to be saved; your own necessity of it; the poors need of it; and Christs command,

Gather

Gather up the fragments that nothing be lost: on the other side you must consider, how far it will hinder your spiritual benefit and duty; and how far the example may be like to encourage such as will do such things without just cause; And so try which is the way of *Gods honour* and *your own* and *your neighbours good*; and that is the way which you must take (As in the Disciples rubbing the ears of Corn, &c.) For the Rule is, that *your labour is then lawful and a duty, when in the judgement of a truly judicious person, it is like to do more good than hurt; And it is then sinful when it is like to do more hurt than good.* Though all cannot discern this, yet (as far as I know) this is the true rule, to judge such actions by. As for them that suppose our Lords day to be under the same Laws of Rest with the Jewish Sabbath, and so think that they have a readyer way to decide these doubts, I will not contend with them, but I have told you why I am not of their mind.

V. From hence I further conclude, that whereas there are some actions which bring some *little benefit*, but yet are no apparent hinderances of any of the work of the day, it seemeth to me too much Ceremoniousness, and too ungospel-like, to trouble our own or other mens Consciences, by concluding such things to be unlawful. If one have a word to speak of some considerable worldly business, which may be forgotten if it be not presently spoken; or if I meet one with whom I must speak the next day about some worldly business, and if I then wish him not to come speak with me, I must send a great way to him afterwards, I will not say that it is a sin to speak such a word. I will first look at a mans positive duties on the Lords day, how he heareth, and readeth, and prayeth, and spendeth his time, and how he instructeth and helpeth his Family; And if he be diligent in seeking God, (*Heb.* 11. 6.) and ply his Heavenly business, I shall be very backward to judge him for a word or action about worldly things that falls in on the by without any hinderance to his spiritual work. And if another speak not a word of any common thing, and yet do little in spiritual things, for his own or others edification, I shall think him a great abuser or neglecter of the Lords day. A few words about a common thing that falleth in the way, may be spoken without any hinderance of any holy duty: But still we must see that it be not a scandalous temptation to others. If I see a man that unexpectedly findeth some uncomely hole or rent in his Cloaths, either pin it up, or sew it up before he goeth abroad, I will not blame him: But if he do it so as to embolden another who useth needlesly to mend his Cloaths on the Lords day, it will be a sin of scandal. If I see one cut some undecent stragling haires before he go forth, I will not blame him: But if he do it before one who will be encouraged by it, to be barbed needlesly on that day, he will offend. And so in other cases.

VI. By these same Rules also we may judge of *Recreations* on the *Lords day*. The Recreations of the mind must be the various holy employments

ployments of the day. No bodily Recreations are lawful which needlesly waste time, or hinder our duty, or divert our minds from holy things, or are a snare to others. Unless it be some weak persons whose health requireth bodily motion, few persons need any other than holy recreations on that day. I know no one man that so much needeth it as my self, who these twenty years cannot digest one dayes meat, unless I walk, or run, or exercise my body before it, till I am hot or sweat; And therefore necessity requireth me to walk or fast: But I do it privately on that day, lest I tempt others to sin. But I will not censure one whom I see walking at fit houres, when for ought I know he may be taken up in some fruitful Meditation: But if persons will walk in the Streets or Fields in idleness, or for vain delight, or discourse, as if the day were too long for them, and they had no business to do for their souls; this is not only a sin, but a very ill sign of one that is senseless of his souls necessity and his duty.

VII. To read History, Philosophy, or common things, unnecessarily on the Lords day, is a sinful diversion from the more spiritual work of it; and unsuitable to the appointed uses of the day (much more Romances, Play Books, or idle stories:) Yea or those parts of *Divinity it self*, which are less practical and useful to the raising of Thankful and Heavenly affections. But yet sometimes such other matter may fall in, at a Sermon, or Conference, or in Meditation, which will require a present satisfaction in some point

point of History, Philosophie, or controversal Divinity, which may be subserviently used to Edification, without sin. Here therefore we must judge prudently.

VIII. A thing that may be lawful singly in it self, unless it be of great necessity is unlawful when he that serveth us in it is drawn or encouraged to make a trade of it. As to use a Barber to cut your hair; or a Tailor to mend your Cloaths, or a Coblar to mend your Shooes: Because if *you* may use him; so may others as well as you, and so he will follow his Calling on the Lords day. And yet I dare not say, if when you are to travel to Church, you find your Shooes or Boots by breaking something, to make you uncapable of going out, but you may get them mended privately, where it may be done without this inconvenience. And though Cooks and Bakers should not be *unnecessarily* used in their trade, yet is it not *alwaies* unlawful, but sometimes very well. Because as *one servant* in the *Kitchin* may be used to dress meat for *all the family*, so one *Baker* or *Cooke* may serve *many families*, and save ten times as many persons the labour which else they must be at; And perhaps with easier and quicker dispatch than others. The trade of the Apothecary, Surgeon and Physician is ordinarily used but for necessity.

IX. There is no sufficient avoidance of such abuses, but by careful foresight, and prevention and preparation the week before; which therefore must be conscionably done.

CHAP.

CHAP. XII.

Of what importance the due Observation of the Lords day is.

THese singular benefits of keeping the Lords day aright, should make all that Love God, or holiness or the Church, or their own or other mens souls, take heed how they grow into a neglect or abuse of it; much more that they plead not for such negligence or abuse.

I. The due observation of the Lords day is needful to *keep up the solemn worship of God, and publick owning and honouring him* in the world: If all men were left to themselves, what time they would bestow in the worshipping of God, the greatest part would cast off all, and grow into Atheisme or utter prophaneness; And the rest would grow into confusion. And if all Princes and Rulers or Churches in the world were left to their own wills to appoint the people on what dayes to meet, some Kingdoms and Churches would have one day, in eight, or nine, or ten, or twenty, and some only now and then an hour, and some one day, and some another, and some next to none at all. For there is no one universal Monarch on Earth to make Laws for them all

all (whatever the Pope or his nominal-General Councils may pretend to :) And they would never all come to any reasonable agreement voluntarily among themselves. Therefore the Light of Nature telleth us, that as a day is meet and needful to be stated, so it is meet that God himself the true Universal Monarch should determine of it; which accordingly he hath done. And this is the very hedge and defensative of Gods publick Worship. When he hath made a Law that *one whole day in seven* shall be spent in it, men are engaged to attend it.

O what a happy acknowledgement of God our Creatour and Redeemer is it, and an honouring of his blessed name, when all the Churches throughout all the World, are at once praising the same God, with the same praises, and hearing and learning the same Gospel, and professing the same faith, and thankfully commemorating the same benefits ! The Church is then indeed, like an Army with Banners. And were it not for *this dayes* observation, alas, how different would the case be ? And what greater thing can man be bound to, than thus, to keep up the solemn acknowledgement and worship of God and our Redeemer in the world ?

II. The due Sanctification of the Lords day, doth tend to *make Religion Universal*, as to Countreys and individual persons, which else would be of narrower extent. When all the world are under a Divine obligation, to spend one day every week in the exercises of Religion, (and superiours see to the performance of their subjects

jects obedience to this Law,) it will make men to be in some sort Religious whether they will or not: Though they cannot be *truly* Religious against their will, it will make them *visibly religious*. Yea Gods own Law, if mans did nothing, would lay an awe on the Consciences of most, who believe that there is a God that made that Law. And the weekly Assemblies keep up the knowledge and profession of the Christian faith, and keep God and Heaven in the peoples remembrance, and keep sin under constant rebukes and disgrace: And were it not for this, Heathenisme, Infidelity and prophaneness would quickly overspread the world. The Lords day keepeth up the Christian Religion in the World.

III. The lamentable *Ignorance* of the *generality* in the world, doth require the strict and diligent observation of the whole Lords day. *Children and Servants*, and ordinary *Countrey people*, yea and too many of *higher* quality, are so exceeding Ignorant of the things of God and their Salvation, that all the constantest diligence that can be used with them, in Preaching, Exhorting, Catechizing, *&c.* will not overcome it with the most. The most diligent Masters of Families lament it, how Ignorant their Families are when they have done the best they can. Let those that plead for dancing and sporting away much of the day, but do like men that do not secretly scorn Christianity, nor despise their servants souls, and let them but try what measure of knowledge the bare hearing of Common Prayer;

Prayer, yea and a Sermon or two with it, will beget in their servants, if the rest of the day be spent in sports; and let them judge according to experience. If ever knowledge be propagated to such, and families made fit to live like Christians, it is likest to be by the holy improvement of this day, in the diligent teaching and Learning the substance of Religion, and in the Sacred exercises thereof.

IV. The great Carnality, Wordliness and Carelesness of the most, and their great aversenes to the things of God, doth require that they be called and kept to a close and diligent improvement of the Lords day. Whatever unexperienced or carnal persons may pretend, that such constant duty so long together will make them worse and more averse, reason, experience and Scripture are all against them. If there be some backwardness at the first, it is not sports and idleness that will cure it; but resisting of the slothful humour, and keeping to the work. For there is that *in Religion* that tendeth to overcome mens *averseness* to Religion; And it must be overcome by *Religion*, and not by *playing* or *idleness*, if ever it be overcome. It is want of knowledge and experience of it, which maketh them loath it or be weary of it: when they have *tryed* it more and *know it* better, they will (if ever) be reconciled to it. Six dayes in a Week are a sufficient diversion. Apprentices, and Pupils and School-boyes will hold on in learning, though they be averse; And you think not all the six dayes too much to hold them to it.

A

A School-boy must learn daily, eight or nine hours in a day; and yet some wretched men (yea Teachers) would perswade poor souls that must learn how to be saved or perish for ever, that less than eight hours one day in seven, is too much to be spent in the needfullest, excellentest and pleasantest matters in all the World.

If you say that the *sublimity* or *difficulty* maketh it wearisome, I answer, that Philosophers do much longer hold on in *harder* speculations.

If you say *Divinity* being unsuitable to carnal minds, their sick Stomachs must take no more than they can digest, I answer, 1. Cannot a Carnal Preacher for his gain, and honour, and fancy, hold on all the year in the study even of Divinity, perhaps eight or ten hours every day in the week? And may not ignorant people be brought *one day* to endure to be taught as long? 2. That which you call *Digesting*, is but *Understanding*, and *believing*, and *receiving* it: And one truth tendeth to introduce another; And he that cannot learn with an hours labour may learn more in two. 3. And it is hearing and exercise that must cure their want of appetite. Experience telleth us, that when people take the liberty of playes, and sports, and idleness for a recreation, they come back with much more want of Love to holy exercises, than they that continue longer at them. Gratifying sloth and sensuality, increaseth it, and increaseth an averseness to all that is good; For who are more averse than they that are most voluptuous? If ever

people

people be made seriously holy, it is a due observation of the whole Lords day, that is like to bring them to it (I mean observing it in such *Learning* and *seeking* duties as they are capable of, till they can do better) For when the mind *long dwelleth* on the *truth*, it will sink in and work; And many strokes will drive the nail to the head.

Let the Adversaries of this day and diligence but observe, And if true experience tell not the World that more souls are Converted on the Lords dayes than on all other dayes besides, and that *Religion best prospereth* both as to the *Number* and the *knowledge* and *serious Holiness* of the professours of it, where the Lords day is carefully sanctified, rather than where Idleness and playing do make intermission, than I will confess that I am uncapable of knowing any thing of this nature by experiences. But if it be so, fight not against the common light.

V. The *Poverty, Servitude* and *worldly necessities* of the most, do require a strict observation of the whole Lords day. *Tenants*, and *Labourers*, *Carters* and *Carryers*, and abundance of Tradesmen are so poor, that they can hardly spare any other considerable proportion of time: much less all their Children and Servants, whose *subjection*, with their Parents and Masters *poverty*, restraineth them. Alas, they are fain to rise early and hasten to their work, and scarce have leisure to eat and sleep as nature requireth: And they are so toiled and wearied with hard labour, that if they have at night a quarter of an hour

l a Chapter and Pray, they can scarce
ieir eyes from sleeping. What time
iister then to come and teach them
uch Ministers again as would be at
do it?) And what time have they to
i? You must teach them on the Lords
ely at all. Almost all that they must
ie *then* learnt.

t but in those former years, when the
me not to Preach the Gospel, the
to me on the week day, house by
also that they Learned much in their
hey were working. But, 1. It came
lies turn but one hour, or little more
Year (For about fourteen families
techized and instructed, did no soon-
t course about.) 2. And our people
Weavers, whose labour was not like
is, Masons, Carpenters, Carryers, *&c.*
eir thoughts; but they could lay a
them and read, or meditate, or
Edification whilest they were work-
this is not the case of the Multi-

y sober man but consider, whether
so ignorant and averse as the most
e be never so diligent on the Lords
dayes intermission be not a great
ection, and a great delayer of their
owledge; when they are like by
to forget all that they had learned
day. What then would these poor
to, if the Lords day it self must be
or played away?

L   V I. The

VI. The tyranny of many Masters maketh the Lords day a great mercy to the world: For if God had not made a Law for their Rest and Liberty, abundance of worldly impious persons, would have allowed them little *Rest* for their bodies, and less opportunity for the good of their souls. Therefore they have cause with great thankfulness to improve the *holy liberty* which God hath given them, and not cast it away on play or idleness.

VII. The full improvement of the Lords dayes doth tend to breed and keep up an able faithful Ministry in the Churches (on which the preservation and glory of Religion much dependeth.) When there is a *necessity of full Ecclesiastical performances* imposed on Ministers, they are also necessitated to prepare themselves with answerable *abilities* and fitness. But when no more is required of them, but to read the Liturgie, or to say a short and dry Discourse, they that know no more is necessary (to their ends) are so strongly tempted to get ability and preparations for no more, that few will overcome the temptation. And therefore the World knoweth that in *Moscovy, Abassia,* and for the most part of the Greek and Armenian Churches, as nothing or little more than Reading is required, so little more ability than to Read is laboured after; And the Ministers are ordinarily so ignorant and weak, as is the scorn and decay of the Christian Religion.

VIII. Yea

VIII. Yea it will strongly encline Masters of Families to labour more for abilities, to instruct and Catechise their Families, and pray with them, and guide them in the fear of God, when they know that the whole day must be improved to the spiritual good of their Families. And so knowledge, abilities, and family-holiness will increase: Whereas those that think themselves under no such obligations, what ignorant, profane and ungodly families have they? because for the most part, they are such themselves.

IX. A multitude of gross sins will be prevented by the due observation of the Lords day. Nothing more usual than for the sports, riots, idleness and sensuality of that day, to be nurseries of Oathes, Curses, Ribaldry, Fornication, Gluttony, Drunkenness, Frayes and Bloodshed. And is not Gods Service better work than these?

X. Lastly, This holy order and prosperity of the Churches, and this knowledge and piety in individual Subjects, will become the safety, beauty, order and felicity, of Kingdomes, and all Civil societies of men. For when the people are fit but duly to use and sanctifie the Lords day, they are fit to use all things in a sanctified manner, and to be an honour to their Countrey, and an ease, and comfort to their Governours, and a common blessing to all about them.

CHAP. XIII.

What other Church Festivals or separated daies are lawful.

I Shall conclude this Discourse with the brief answer of this Question.

I. No sober Christian doubteth, but that some part of every day is to be spent in Religious exercises; And that even our earthly business must be done with a spiritual intent and mind. And that every day must be kept as *like* to the Lords day, as our weakness, and our other duties, which God hath laid upon us, will allow.

II. Few make any question but the whole dayes of *Humiliation* and of *Thanksgiving* may and must be kept upon great and extraordinary occasions, of Judgements or of mercies. And that many Churches may agree in these. And I know no just reason why the Magistrate may not (with Charity and Moderation to the weak) impose them, and command such an agreement among his Subjects.

III. Few doubt but the Commemoration of great *Mercies* or *Judgements* may be made *anniversary*

versary, and of long continuance. As the Powder-plot day (*Nov.* 5.) is now made among us, to preserve the memorial of that deliverance. And why may it not be continued, whilest the great sense of the benefit should be continued? And so the second of *Sept.* is set apart for the Anniversary humbling remembrance, of the Firing of *London*. And so in divers other cases.

IV. The great blessing of an Apostolick Ministry, and of the stability of the Martyrs in their sufferings for Christ, being so rare and notable a Mercy to the Church, I confess I know no reason why the Churches of all succeeding ages may not keep an Anniversary day of Thanksgiving to God for *Peter* or *Paul*, or *Stephen*, as well as for the Powder plot-deliverance. I know not where God hath forbidden it, directly or indirectly. If his instituting the *Lords day* were a virtual prohibition for man to separate any more, or if the prohibition of *adding* to Gods Word were against it, they would be against other daies of Humiliation and Thanksgiving, especially Anniversarily; which we confess they are not. If the reason be scandal, lest the *Men* should have the honour instead of God, I Answer, 1. An honour is due to Apostles and Martyrs in their places, in meet subordination to God. 2. Where the case of scandal is notorious, it may become by that accident unlawful, and yet not be so in other times and places.

L. 3   V. The

V. The Devil hath here been a great *Undoer* by *Overdoing*: When he knew not how else to cast out the holy observation of the Lords day, with zealous people he found out the trick of deviling so many dayes called *Holy dayes* to set up by it, that the people might perceive that the observation of them all as *holy*, was never to be expected. And so the Lords day was jumbled in the heap of *holy dayes*, and all turned into Ceremony, by the Papists and too many other Churches in the World. Which became *Calvins* temptation (as his own words make plain) to think too meanly of the Lords day with the rest.

VI. In the lawful observation of daies, it is most orderly to do as the Churches do which we live among and are to joine with.

VII. But if Church tyranny would overwhelm any place with over-numerous daies (or Ceremonies) which are (singly considered) lawful, we should do nothing needlesly to countenance and encourage such usurpation.

VIII. Yet is it lawful to hear a Sermon, which shall be Preached on a humane *Holy day*, which is imposed by Usurpation. Seeing such a Moral duty may be done, and so great a benefit received, without any approbation of the inconvenient season.

IX. And when we think it unlawful to joyne
in

or contempt, or working upon that day ? And so *Paul* justifieth himself against the Jews accusations, that they *found him not in the Temple disputing with any man, nor raising up the people, nor in the Synagogues, nor in the City,* Act. 24. 12. unless it be when we have a special call, to reprove the errour which we forbear complying with.

X. It is long agoe decided by the Holy Ghost, *Rom.* 14. *&* 15. that we must not be contentious, contemptuous, nor censorious against one another, about things of no greater moment, than the Jewish *dayes* were, though some observed them without just cause: Because the Kingdom of God consisteth not in Meats, and Drinks, and Daies, but *in righteousness and peaceableness and joy in the Holy Ghost. And he that in these things serveth Christ, is acceptable to God (and received by him) and approved of (wise) men, and should be received to Communion with them,* Rom. 14. 17, 18. *&* 15. 7. We must therefore *follow after the things that make for peace, and things wherewith one may edifie another*, Rom. 14. 19.

XI. The Controversie, whether it be lawful to separate an Anniversary day for the Commemoration of Christs Nativity, Circumcision and such like things which were equally existent in the

Apostles dayes, and the reason for observing them equal with following times, (and so the Apostles had the same reason to have appointed such dayes had they thought it best, as we have) I acknowledge too hard for me to determine: not being able to prove it lawful, I cannot own and justifie it; And not seeing a plain prohibition I will not condemn it, nor be guilty of unpeaceable opposing Church Customes or Authority in it, but behave my self as a peaceable doubter.

XII. But that no earthly power may appoint a *weekly day*, in commemoration of any part of our Redemption, besides the Lords day, and so make another separated weekly stated Holy day, I think plainly unlawful, Because it is a doing the same thing for one day which God hath done already by another; And so seemeth to me, 1. An usurpation of a power not given, and 2. An accusation of Christ and the Holy Ghost, as if he had not done his work sufficiently, but man must come after and do it better.

But especially if such (or any day or Ceremony) be by an universal Law imposed on the Universal Church, it is arrogant usurpation of the Divine Authority; there being no Vicarious Head or Monarch under Christ of all the World or all the Church, nor any Universal Governour who may exercise such Legislation, whether personal or Collective.

The same I may say of any that would presume to abrogate the Lords day.

And so much shall suffice in great haste of this subject. And

And to thee O moſt Glorious and Gracious Creatour and Redeemer, I humbly return my unfeigned thanks, for the unſpeakable mercies which I have received on thy day ; And much more for ſo great a Mercy to all thy Churches and the World : And craving the pardon (among the reſt) of the ſins which I have committed on thy Day, I beſeech thee to continue this exceeding mercy, to thy Churches and to Me ; and reſtore me and other of thy Servants, to the priviledges, and comforts of this Day ; which we have forfeited and loſt; And let me ſerve thee in the Life, and Light, and Love of thy Spirit, in theſe thy Holy Dayes on Earth, till I be prepared for, and received to, the Everlaſting Reſt in Heavenly Glory, *Amen.*

Octob. 11.
1670.

FINIS.

AN APPENDIX

For further Confirmation of Gods own Separation of the *Lords day*, and Disproving the Continuation of the Jewish *Seventh day Sabbath*.

Written since the Treatise went to the Press, upon the Invitations of some latter Objections.

Heb. 7. 12. *For the Priesthood being changed, there is made of necessity a change also of the Law.*

2 Cor. 3. 7, 11. *But if the Ministration of Death, in Letters Engraven in Stones was glorious, &c. If that which was done away was glorious, much more that which remaineth is glorious.*

Act. 15. 28. *It seemed good to the Holy Ghost and to us, to lay upon you no greater Burden than these necessary things—*

Col. 2. 16. *Let no man judge you in Mat, or in Drink, or in respect of an Holy day, or of the New Moon, or of the Sabbath, which are a shadow of things to come, but the Body is of Christ.*

LONDON,
Printed for *Nevil Simmons*, at the three Crowns near *Holborn* Conduit. 1671.

(157)

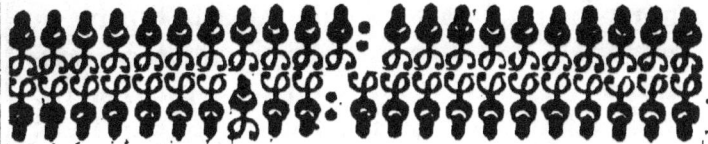

CHAP. I.

An Answer to certain Objections against the Lords Day.

Hough they are answered before, the Reader must pardon me, if upon the particular urgencies of some Objectors, I again make answer to these that follow.

Obj. Act. 20. 7. *The first day of the Week ; Gr.* [*one of the Sabbaths*] *That the breaking of Bread there was common Eating, compare the like greek phrase,* Act. 27. 35. &c. v. 42. *see* Esa. 58. 7. *However it was but an example of Preaching, and breaking Bread, upon a special occasion.*

Answ. 1. That Ἐν τῇ μιᾷ τῶν σαββάτων signifieth on the *first day* of the *week*, the Generality of the ancients both Greek and Latine agree, whose testimony about the sense of a word, is the best Dictionary and evidence that we can expect. And the same phrase used of the Day of Christs Resurrection by the Evangelists proveth it. Though I am sorry to hear of one that denyeth that also, and asserteth that Christ rose on the
seco nd

second day morning, because else he could not as *to wit, be these days and nights*, buried. But I am not so proud as to think my self capable of convincing that man in such a matter of fact, who will not believe the historical witness of the whole Church of Christ, and expecteth to be believed against them all, at such a distance in the end of the World.

2. There is no doubt but that κλάσις τῦ ἄρτε, breaking of Bread, was both a *Common* and a *Sacred* action: And the phrase is to be interpreted by the context, to know when it signifieth the *common*, and when the *Sacred*. In *Act.* 27. 35. the context teacheth us to interpret it of communicating: But that it doth not so *Act.* 2. 42, 46. or *Act.* 20. is plain to him that considereth. 1. That it was then usual to communicate Sacramentally in all their Church Assemblies. 2. That these mentioned were *Church-assemblies*; the *Church* being met purposely for Sacred works. Yet it is to be remembred, that the *Love-feasts* did usually concurr in the beginning with the Sacrament, and the name might be used with respect to both.

3. That it was not a meer occasional meeting, is apparent to the unprejudiced. 1. Because they stayed at *Troas* seven dayes, *v.* 6. and in all the seven make no mention of this exercise, but on one only, which was the first. 2. Because as is said it was not a *family*, or *by-meeting*, but a *Church-meeting*; [*The Disciples came or assembled together*] 3. Because it is said that they assembled for this very end, to break bread [συνηγμένων τῶν μαθητῶν τῦ κλάσαι ἄρτον.] 4. The great length of time which

which was spent in the holy exercises: Besides the rest of the Worship, and breaking of Bread, *Paul* Preaching till midnight: which intimateth that such work took up the day. 5. Because it is mentioned as a matter of their custome: They did not assemble because *Paul* called them to *hear him* only, as being to depart on the morrow; But *Paul* assembled *with them* at the time of *their assembling to break Bread*; And it seemeth that he deferred his journey for that opportunity. 6. Because other Texts as joyned with this, and infallible Church History following, do prove past all doubt that it was the constant custome of all the Churches so to do.

Obj. 1 Cor. 16. 1, 2. *The first day of the week*, &c. gr. *one of the Sabbaths*. It is an ordinance to lay aside for charitable uses; but not one word about changing of the Sabbath.

Answ. The abolition of the Sabbath we prove not by this Text, but by others: All that we bring *this* for, is but to shew in conjunction with others, as part of the Sacred History, that the first day was the Churches separated day. And I pray mark the strength of the proof, that the Apostle did [*give order that all the Churches of Galatia as well as the Corinthians, should deposite*] their Almes on one and the same day, *viz.* on the first day: Was it not enough to tie them to the *contribution*, but he must tie them all *to one set day to lay* it by, or deposite it? if it had not been because the Churches used to assemble on this day, and not to appear before God empty (as Dr. *Hammond* noteth on the Text?) Whoever heard else that God or man tyed several Countreys

treys to one set day for the private depositing of their own moneys afterward to be distributed? *With such Sacrifices God is well pleased*; And therefore it was ever accounted by Christians a fit work for the sanctified day: But no other day was ever appointed peculiarly for the set time of laying by mens gifts of Charity.

Obj. Rev. 1. 10. John *was in the Spirit on the Lords day*. Compare Exod. 20. 10, &c. Esa. 58. 13, &c. Luk. 6. 5. Mark 2. 28. Mat. 12. 8, &c. *And if the Scriptures be the rule to judge, resolve whether that day be not the Lords day, of which day, (and of which only as distinguished from the other dayes of the week,) the Son of man is Lord.*

Answ. We are not upon a Controversie of *title* or *propriety*, whether God *be Lord* of other dayes: For so no doubt, he is *Lord of all*, and therefore no more of one than another, because his propriety in each one is *absolute*; And it can be no more in any. Thus also he is absolute Lord of all things, all places, all persons, &c. And yet some things, some places, some persons have been *separated to his service* by a peculiar Dedication and Relation; and thence have been peculiarly called *The Lords*. And the Texts cited by you out of the old Testament prove that such was the seventh day Sabbath then: But not that it is so now; or was to be so for perpetuity.

And the words of the new Testament cited [*The Son of man is Lord also, or even of the Sabbath day,*] shews no more, then that it was in his power: He giveth it as a reason for his doing that which the Pharises counted Sabbath-breaking (By which he oftentimes offended them;) and

and not as a reason of his *establishing* it. And it seemeth plainly to mean, that *being* but a *Positive Law*, and a *Law of Moses*, he had power to change it, and dispense with it, as well as with other *Positives* and *Mosaical Laws*. As it is said, Ephes. 1. 22, 23. *he hath made him Head over all things to the Church*; not *Head to all things*; so he is *Lord over, or of all dayes*; But all are not *separated* to his Worship. As it is said, Joh. 17. 2. *As thou hast given him power over all flesh, that he should give eternal life to as many as thou hast given him*: so it may be said, he hath power over all dayes, that he may sanctifie one to his peculiar service, and use the rest in more common works.

But that which we bring this text for is but to know what day is notified to the world by this title of *The Lords day*, and consequently was then accounted his *separated peculiar* day. Now the signification of words is known but by use: They are not *Natural* signes, but *Arbitrary*: You know not the sense of one word of Hebrew, Greek, or Latine, but by the History of their use, by Dictionaries, Authors or other Tradition. Now it is unquestionable to any man verst in antiquity, that all the Churches, and Authors, Greek and Latine, Syriack, Æthiopick, Persian, Arabick, that have been known among us, and speak of such things, do unanimously call the first day of the week by the name of the *Lords day*, as being so called from the beginning, even from the Apostles; And all old expositors so interpret this present Text. And you may as well question what day the word *Sabbath* signified in the Old Testament almost

almost, as what day the name of [*The Lords day*] signified in the new; Or what sort of people they were that were called *Christians* first at *Antioch*, when only one sort hath ever since been notified by that name; Even the Disciples of Christ. The Greek, with the Syriack Translation, the Arabick, the vulgar Latine, have all [*The Lords day;*] and the Ethiopick as equipollent, hath [*the first day*] And Dr. *Heylin* (who would find something against it if any thing were to be found) speaking of some of late that otherwise expound it, is so ingenious as to say (Par. 2. cap. 1. p. 37.) *Touching this we will not meddle: Let them that own it look to it: The rather since St. John hath generally been expounded in the other sense, by Aretas, and Andr. Cæsariensis on the place, and by Bedæ de rat. temp. c. 6. and by the suffrage of the Church, the best expositor of the word of God; wherein this day hath constantly since the time of the Apostles been honoured with that name above other daies*] And I know no one man (nor many) that at 1600 years distance almost, is so worthy to be believed for the bare sense of a word, as the constant use and universal testimony of all ages from that time till now.

As Christ is the Lord of all our Suppers, yet all are not named The *Lords* Supper; so is it in this case.

I must needs conclude therefore, that if I should cast off the evidence of this Text, upon no greater reason than you offer me, I think, I should resist the holy Ghost, and use violence against Gods word which I should obey.

Obj.

Obj. *There is no Law in the Scripture to observe the first day, no promise made to observers of it, no threatning against the breakers of it,* &c. *shew it. And if no Law, no transgression,* Rom. 4. 15. *Sin is a transgression of the Law.*

Answ. I have shewed you full proof of a Law for it before. Though it is not Chrifts way to enact his Laws in that Majeſtick Commanding form as God did to *Moſes* on the Mount: But as he condeſcended into flesh, to be a Teacher and Saviour, in the form of a Servant, under the Law himſelf, to redeem thoſe that were under it, ſo he maketh his Laws in a merciful Teaching ſtile. All that is revealed by him as his will appointing our duty is his Law. But that we obſerve the Lords day is revealed by him as his will, making it our duty.

Theſe are his Laws requiring us to Hear and obey his ſpirit in his Apoſtles, Joh. 20. 21, 22. *As the Father hath ſent me, ſo ſend I you: And when he had ſaid this, he breathed on them and ſaid, Receive ye the Holy Ghoſt,* &c. Luk. 10. 16. *He that heareth you, heareth me.*

And this is his Law requiring his Apoſtles by that ſpirit to promulgate his Laws, and make known his will. Mat. 28. 19, 20. Go, diſciple me all Nations, Baptizing them, *&c. Teaching them to obſerve all things whatever I have commanded you, and loe I am with you alwaies to the end of the world* (or age) with the other Texts forecited.

And that the Spirit in the Apoſtles hath ſetled the Lords day, as the ſeparated day for holy aſſemblies and Worſhip, I have proved to you;

both by the Texts which you now fought in vain to make void, and by the unqueſtionable practice and hiſtory of the univerſal Church, from that age untill this. And withal by other Texts which you omit: which (not alone, but) all ſet together make up the proof, becauſe it is hiſtorical evidence of a matter of fact, which we have to ſeek after.

1. Chriſts Reſurrection laid the foundation, or gave the Cauſe; as Gods ceaſing from his works did of the Sabbath. 2. Chriſts appearing to them aſſembled on that day, began the actual ſeparation. 3. The Holy Ghoſt coming down on them, on that day, did more notably ſanctifie it. 4. The Holy Ghoſt as an infallible ſpirit in them, did cauſe them to make a publick ſettlement of that day in all the Churches, which was the full and actual eſtabliſhment. 5. This ſettlement is fully proved *de facto* in Scripture and infallible hiſtory. 6. And that there are promiſes and threatnings, to the obeyers and rejecters, of Chriſts commands, (whom the Father commanded us to hear, and who is the great Prophet of the Church,) I hope you believe. Rev. 20. 14. *Happy are they who do his commandments that they may have right to the tree of life,* &c. Heb. 12. 25. *See that yee refuſe not him that ſpeaketh; For if they eſcaped not who refuſed him that ſpake on earth, much more,* &c. Act. 3. 23. *It ſhall come to paſs that every ſoul that will not hear that Prophet, ſhall be deſtroyed from among the people:* 1 Joh. 4. 6. *We are of God: He that knoweth God heareth us: he that is not of God, heareth not us: Hereby know we the ſpirit of truth, and the ſpirit of Errour.*

If

If besides all this you must have *particular precepts, promises and threatnings* in the form which you imagine to be fittest, you may for want of those deny many other Gospel Laws as well as this. Have you not much more for the separation of the Lords day, than you have for *Infants Baptism*, for a *Christian Magistrate*, for *Christians wageing Warr*, for *prohibited degrees as to Marriage*, &c.

I am perswaded the sober study of these points would do much to convince the contrary minded.

1. How much of Chrifts work as to the settlement of Church-Orders, was committed to the *Apostles* to be done, and how little he publickly setled himself in person, before his Resurrection.

2. How much the Gospel administration excelleth that of the Law. And what eminent Glory God designeth to himself by the work of mans Redemption, and how much more now he calleth man to Read, and Study and Know him in the face of Jesus Christ, than in the Creation, And how largely the change of the *Covenant* is proved in the Epistle to the Hebrews.

3. What a change is made herein as to mans duty, since the fall of man under the *wrath* of the *Creator*, who is not now his *Rest*, but his *terrour* and a *consuming fire*, till Reconciled and Adopting us in Chrift; And since the *Earth is cursed* to us as a punishment for our sins.

4. How much of the certainty, and Glory of the Christian faith, and of all our Rest and Consolation in it, is laid in the Gospel on the RESURRECTION of our Lord, as beginning

ginning a new World, or Creation as it were, and as conquering and triumphing over death and Satan, and sealing the promise and bringing Life and Immortality to Light, and opening the Kingdom of Heaven to Believers.

5. How much of Christs Legislation, and administration of his Church-settlement and Government was to be done by the *Holy Ghost!* And how glorious this office of the *Holy Ghost* is, and of what grand importance to be understood: As he was the promised Paraclete or *Advocate* or *Agent* of our glorified Lord, to do his Work on Earth in his bodily absence; To whom the Infallibility of the Scriptures, the sealing operation of Miracles, the Sanctification of Believers, and forming them for Glory in the Image of God, is to be ascribed: Whom to *Blaspheme* is the *unpardonable sin.*

6. How dangerous a thing it is made by the Holy Ghost to seek to *set up* Moses *Law*, (as the whole Epistle to the *Gal:* besides most of the other Epistles testifie) as intimating a denyal of Christ, and a falling from Grace, and a perverse setting up of that which Christ came to take down, as part of our own redemption. And how large and plain *Paul* is upon this Subject; and how the *Spirit* in all the Apostles did determine it, *Act.* 15. And how the *Cerinthians, Nicolaitans, Ebionites, Nazareans,* and many more of the condemned Heresies of that age, which troubled the Churches, and whom the Apostles wrote against, went all that way of mingling the Jewish Law with the Gospel.

7. How

7. How plainly and expresly *Paul* numbreth *Sabbaths* with the shaddows that cease, *Col.* 2. 16. (to pass by other Texts) And what violence mens own wits must use, in denying the evidence of so plain a Text. Their reason, that he saith not *Sabbath* but *Sabbaths*, is against themselves; the plural number being most comprehensive, and other Sabbaths receiving their name from this; And the word *Sabbath* alwaies used in Scripture, for a Rest which was partly Ceremonial. See what Dr. *Young* in his excellent *Dies Domin* saith of this Text (Though I know some say otherwise to the injury of their own cause,]

8. How many years together the Churches had been in possession, and consequently in the undoubted knowledge, of the true established day of holy Worship, before a word of the New Testament was Written. And therefore that it was not written to be the first enacting of this day or change; but for other uses.

9. And yet how much evidence of the fact there is in the Scripture it self, that really such a day was used for the ordinary Church-assemblies, as a peculiar separated day; even by the Common *order* of the Apostles in the Churches, as 1 *Cor.* 16. 1, 2. speaks.

10. And how impossible it is that all the Churches in the World should from their beginning keep this as the separated day, even by the Apostles and from their times, if it had not been so ordered by them indeed. And whether it be possible that in no age neer the original hereof, no Pastor, no Christian, no Heretick, no Enemy would have detected the fraud or common Errour,

Errour, or once have written, that this day was not separated or used by the Apostles or Apostolical Churches; no nor any one (that I know of, that denyed not the Resurrection) ever to have scrupled or opposed the day.

11. Whether they that can reject such Historical evidence as this is, do not unwittingly cast away the *holy Scriptures*, what zeal soever they pretend or have for their honour and perfection.

12. Whether they that can reject all this evidence, and yet can find in the second Commandment, the prohibition of all formes of Prayer, Sermons, Catechismes, & all modal inventions of men, as Images, if not Idols, are *without partiality*, or do not walk as men, by very different measures, and partial conceptions.

I would on my knees intreat some most dear and worthy friends, on their knees to ponder these twelve particulars.

But because by their preterition of the Text, *Act.* 2. 1, 2. I perceive they observe not, that the Holy Ghost came down on the Lords day, Let them consider that the Passeover was on the Sabbath day that year, and therefore it must needs be just fifty dayes to that Lords day, and it must be the day of Pentecost.

And it is not a trifle, that the first Sermon to the people was Preached by *Peter* on that day, and 3000 Converted by it and Baptized.

Dr. *Heylins* own words are these, [Part. 2. p. 13. *The first particular passage which did occurr in holy Scripture touching the first day of the week, is that upon that day the Holy Ghost did*

first

first come down on the Apostles, and that on the same day St. Peter *Preached his first Sermon, to the* Jews, *and Baptized such as believed, there being added to the Church that day* 3000 *souls*] And to prove the day he saith, p. 14. [*The rule being this, that on what day soever the second of the* Passover *did fall, on that also fell the great Feast of* Pentecost (as Scaliger de Emend. Temp. l. 2.) *So that as often as the* Passover *did fall on the Sabbath, as this year it did, then* Pentecost *fell on the Sunday.*]

The last part of our Objections are from History; and it is said,

Obj. [Qu. *Whether the observation of the first day was not brought into this Island by* Antichrist, *about* 408 *or* 409 *years agoe?* Roger Hoveden *about an.* 1202 (*above* 1200 *years after* Christ) *mentioneth a Council held in* Scotland *for the initiation or first bringing in that which he calls the Dominical day: see this testimony mentioned by* Binius *in his Councils, and somewhat enlarged by* Matth. Paris *the old impression fol.* 192, 193. *and the last Edition fol.* 200 *and* 201; *And how the King of* England *and the Nobility would not then receive this alteration.* —— *I conceive that in the first Centuries the great Controversie relating to this was about translating the keeping the* Passover, *which they now call* Easter, *from the fourteenth day of the first Moon,* &c. (*under the colour of honouring* Christ) *to the first day of the* Week *as the Dominical day; which the* Popes *first set themselves with great vehemency to introduce* —— *And as the* Pope *obtained his purpose for one day in a year, so by degrees in some places, came in one day in a week,*

week, the *first day to be observed*, and the *seventh day* by one of the Popes turned from a Festival to a Fast, whilest many of the Eastern and some of the Western Churches did still retain withall the observation of the seventh-day Sabbath together with the first day, and others of the Churches in the East and West kept only to the seventh day as the Christian Sabbath, &c.

Answ. How much more desirable an Adversary is *Heylin* by his acquaintance with History! 1. Were any of the Authors I before cited either Antichristian or 1200 years after Christ?

Ignatius, *if genuine* was about *an.* 102. *If not*, as *Dalæus* thinks then he was about 300.
The Canons called the Apostles, and the Constitutions called the Apostles, very ancient.

Justin Martyr wrote his *Apol*, *an.* 150. about 50 years after St. *Johns* death; where his testimony is as plain as can be spoken. To which *Plinyes* who wrote about 107. some seven years after St. *Johns* death, may be joyned that he may be understood of the day.

Clemens Alexand. about 94 years after St. *John*, *an.* 194.

Tertullian who is most express, and full, and frequent, about 198, that is, 98 years after St. *John*.

Origen about 206 began his Teaching.

Cyprian about *an.* 250.

Athanasius who wrote largely of it, about *an.* 330.

To what purpose should I mention again *Eusebius*, *Greg. Nazianzen*, *Nyssen*, and all the rest. It was but about *an.* 309, that *Constantine* began his

his raign, who made Laws for the Lords day, which other Christian Emperours enlarged. But how much earlier were all those Synods which *Eusebius* mentioned, which in the determination of *Easter* owned the Lords day? And that of *Nice* was but about *an.* 327. The Council of *Laodicea* but about *an.* 314 or 320.

The Council of *Eliberis* about *an.* 307. *Can.* 21. saith, *If any that live in the Cities shall stay from Church three Lords daies, let him be so long suspended from the Sacrament, till he be sensible of his punishment.*

After this how many Councils and how many Imperial Laws take care of the Lords dayes? It is tedious to cite them.

To these may be added, 1. The common agreement that it is founded in the *Resurrection*, and was *from that time.* 2. The early contest for keeping *Easter* only on that day, which you note, as being a day by all Christians received. 3. The common detestation of *Fasting* on that day. 4. And the universal custome of *not kneeling* in adoration on that day: which all shew that the day was specially observed.

Athanasius saith de sab. & Circ. *Even as at the first it was commanded that the Sabbath should be observed in memory of the finishing of the World, so do we celebrate the Lords day as the commemoration of the beginning of a new Creation.* And Hom. de Sem. *The Lord transferred the Sabbath to the Lords day.* Though *Nannius* question the *Hom. de semente*, so do few others, and none that I know of, question that *de Sab. & Circ.*

Greg.

Greg. Nyss. Orat. in s. Pasc. saith, *As God rested on the Sabbath from all his works which he had done in the Creation, so did the only begotten Son of God rest in truth from all his works,* &c.

August. Epist. 119. *The Lords day was declared to Christians by the Lords Resurrection. From that time* (or thence) *it began to have its Festivity.*

Maximus Taurinensis saith, *Hom.* 3. *de Pentec. The Lords day is therefore set apart because on it our Saviour as the rising Sun, discussing the infernal darkness, did shine forth in his resurrection.*

And for Fasting, *Tertul. de Cor. Mil. c.* 3. saith, *We account it unlawful to fast on the Lords day.* And though the Montanists fasted excessively, they excepted the Lords day, *Tertul. adv. Psych. c.* 15.

Ignatius and the *Apost. Const. & Can.* are forecited of this.

Austin saith, Ep. 86. *It is a great scandal to fast on the Lords day.* (Which the *Manichees* were accused of.)

The *Concil. Gangr. Can.* 18. saith, *If any on pretense of abstinence fast on the Lords day, let him be* Anathema.

The *Concil. Cæsar-august. c.* 2. is against fasting on the Lords day *either for the sake of any time* (as *Lent*) or *perswasion, or superstition whatsoever.* So the *Concil. Agath. c.* 12. *Concil. Aurel.* 4. *c.* 2. And the *Concil. Carth. an.* 398. *Can.* 64. *Let him be taken for no Catholick who purposely fasteth on the Lords day.*

And the prohibition of kneeling in adoration, I have opened before, *ex Concil. Nic. c.* 20. *Concil. Trul. Epiphan. &c.* To which I adde *Collect.*
Can.

Can. Johan. Antioch. sub titulo L. Tertul. de Cor. Mil. c. 3. (now cited) *Hieronym. adv. Lucifer. cap.* 4. *Die dominico & per omnem Pentecosten nec de geniculis adorare, & jejunium solvere, multaque alia quæ non Scripta sunt, rationabilis sibi observatio vindicavit.* (yet *Paul* kneeled, *Act.* 20. in that time, *vid. Justell. ad Can.* 20. *Conc. Nic.*) *Question. ad Orthod. inter Justin. opera qu.* 115. *p.* 283. *Die Dominico genua non flectere symbolum est Resurrectionis,* &c. *Germanus Constantinop. in Theoria Eccles. p.* 149. Our not kneeling on the Lords day, signifieth our erection from our fall, by Christs Resurrection, *&c.* see also *Basil de spir. Sanc. c.* 27. *To.* 2. *p.* 112, 113. *& Balsamon* theron *p.* 1032. *& Zonari. in c.* 20. *Conc. Nic. p.* 66. see *Casp. Suicerus de hisce sacr. observ. c.* 6.

2. Your Historical observations are utterly mistaken. The observation of the Lords day was in all the Churches past all Controversie from the beginning, while the time of *Easter* was in Controversie, as I have proved. Why would you not name those Churches in *East* and *West* (which I never read or heard of) yea or that *person,* that was for the seventh day alone ? I am confident because you could not do it. Indeed all Churches called the seventh day alone by the old name *Sabbath,* while they maintained the Sabbath to be ceased; But under the name of the *Lords day,* the first was solemnly observed.

3. In *Hoveden* and *Mat. Paris,* there is not a word of what you say; so much do you mis-cite History. There is indeed *an.* 1201. (which as I remember is *Hovedens* last) the story that many Authors talk of, and *Heylin* mentioneth, of

one

one that found a Letter pretended from Heaven upon the Altar, reproving the crying sins of the times, and especially the prophanation of the Lords day, and requiring them to keep it strictly for the time to come: which was so far from being the *initiation* of the *Lords* day, that it was about 1167 years after it. And how could men pretend such a Divine reproof for such a sin, if the day not been received before? I pray read *Heylins* History against us, which will set you righter in the matter of fact. And there is no mention of any such Council as you talk of, for the initiation of the Lords day, nor any resistance of the Kings, or Scots: There is nothing of all this in *Hoveden* or *Mat. Paris*.

4. But what if *England* had been ignorant of the Lords day till then (which is utterly untrue) it followeth not that they kept the Sabbath on the seventh day. Nor would a Barbarous remote corner of the World, prejudice the testimony of all Christs Churches in every age.

5. But that you may see how greatly you mistake the case of *England*; read but our eldest English Historian, *Beda Hist. Eccles.* As *l*. 1. 26. he mentioneth an old Church named St. *Martins* built in the Romans time, and *cap.* 33. a Church built by the ancient faithful Romans; (And by the way, I think it most probable that the Roman Souldiers first brought Christianity into *Brittain*) so he oft describeth the Worship as agreeable to other Churches: And *l*. 2. *c*. 2. he begins his reproof of the Britains for not keeping *Easter* on the *due Lords* day, but never reproveth them for not keeping the *Lords day* it self. And though

the

d the Scots had so little regard of
Bishops sent from *Rome*, that they
d so much as to eat with them, yea
the same Inne (*cap. 4. li. 2.*) yet
rds day there was no Controversie.
he tells you that the Scots difference
lay continued till, *an. 716.* for want
:e from other Churches, though
nd his followers were very holy per-
(that you may see your errour) he
u that they did not keep *Easter day*
s *on the fourteenth day still, as some*
n the Lords day; but not in the right
saith he) *they knew. (as being Chri-*
be Lords Resurrection which was on
of the week, *was alwaies to be cele-*
first day of the week ; *But being*
d Rusticks, they had not yet learn-
same first day of the week, which is
Lords day; did come.]
see that it was past Controversie
at the Lords day must be Celebra-
rial of Chrifts Resurrection, and the
iot *Easter* on any other Week day ;
ley had not been like Christians, if
it owned and kept the Lords day ;
I not skill enough in Calculating the
to know when the true Anniversary
came about, but kept *Easter* on a
s day.
he saith again in the praise of *Finan*
. that though he kept not *Easter* at
, yet he did not, *as some falsly think*,
ny *week day in the fourteenth Moon*
with

with the Jews; but he alwayes kept it on the Lords day, from the fourteenth Moon to the twentieth, because of the Belief of the Lords Resurrection, which the Church truly believed was on the first day of the week for the hope of our Resurrection, and which (they believed) will fall out on the same first day, of the week, which is now called the Lords day.

So cap. 25. the King and the Queen kept Easter on several Lords dayes, and the difference made the stir: And *Wilfrid* in his Speech there saith the same, that the Scots kept *Easter* only on the Lords day; (by whom the King at that time was changed.)

And li. 3. c. 26. *Beda* saith that *Tuda*, (another holy follower of the Scots) being made Bishop,

On the Lords daies the people flock by crowds together either to the Church, or to the Monasteries, not to refresh their bodies, but to learn the word of God; and if any Priest hapt to come into a Village, presently the Inhabitants, Congregati in unum, *gathered together, took care to seek from him the word of life.*]

Cap. 2. li. 4. *Theodorus* his Consecration on the Lords day is mentioned.

Lib. 4. cap. 5. In the Synod at *Herudford* the first Canon is that all keep *Easter* on the Lords day next after the fourteenth Moon of the first Month.

Lib. 5. cap. 22. *Ceolfridus* sendeth an Epistle to the King of the *Picts*, in which are these words [*Postquam vero Pascha nostrum immolatus est Christus, Diemque nobis Dominicam, quæ apud antiquos una vel prima Sabbati sive Sabbatorum vocatur,*

vocatur, gaudio suæ Resurrectionis fecit esse solennem; ita hanc nunc Apostolica traditio festis Paschalibus inseruit.] that is, [*But when Christ our Passover was sacrificed for us, and by the Joy of his Resurrection made the Lords day, which by the Ancients was called one or the first of the Sabbath or Sabbaths, to be a solemn day to us; so now Apostolical Tradition hath ingraffed it into the Paschal Festivals:*] Where you see that the Lords day settled as solemn by the Resurrection, he taketh for uncontroverted, but the graffing it into the *Easter* Festivals, he ascribeth to Apostolical Tradition, meaning St. *Peters*.

And after in the same Epistle [*Qui tertia post immolationem suæ passionis die resurgens à mortuis, hanc dominicam vocari, & in eâ nos annuatim Paschalia ejusdem Resurrectionis voluit festa celebrare;*] that is, [*Christ rising from the dead, the third day after the Sacrifice of his passion, would have this called the Lords day, and would have us on it to Celebrate the Paschal Feast of his Resurrection.*] The like is after again in that Epistle, with this addition, that *we hold that our own Resurrection will be on the Lords day.* By this Epistle the King of the *Picts* was brought to Conformity in that day and made Laws for it: And *Cap.* 23. The Scots of *Hy* who stood out so long, were brought to it by the perswasion of *Eigbertus.* Judge now of your Historical note of *England.*

But that you may see more of this, you may Read *Beda's* mind that lived in *England* in other of his Works. On Act 20. [*In una Sabbathi cum convenissemus ad frangendum panem; id est,*

Die Dominico qui est primus a Sabbato, cum ad mysteria celebranda Congregati essemus,] that is, [*On the Lords day, which is the first from the Sabbath, when we were Congregated to Celebrate the Mysteries*]—— And he thinks it called, *The Lords day, because it is the Remembrance of the Lords Resurrection or ours.*

And on, *Luc.* 6. *fol.* 78. he saith [*The observation of the Legal Sabbath, ought of it self to cease, and the natural liberty of a Sabbath to be restored, which till Moses time was like other dayes. That as it is not circumcision or the Ceremonies of the Law that save the Church but the faith of Abraham working by Love, by which being uncircumcised he was justified, so he calleth the second Sabbath after the first, no other but the spiritual Sabbath, in which as on other daies, it is lawful to do any profitable work, for distinction from the Jewish Sabbath, in which it was not lawful to travel, to gather Wood, nor to do other needful things*] Pardon his Errour about that word; I only cite it for the historical use.

And on *Luc.* 24. 1. *fol.* 143. [*One of the Sabbaths, or the first of the Sabbaths, is the first day after the Sabbath, which the Christian custome hath called the Lords day, because of the Lords Resurrection.*]

And ibid. *fol.* 143. [*Whence Ecclesiastical custome hath obtained, that either in memory of Christs Resurrection, or for the hope of ours, we Pray not with bended knees, but only with faces declined towards the Earth, on every Lords day, and all the* quadragesimæ.]

And in *Act.* 2. 1. [*The Holy Ghost sent——the example*

example of the ancient sign returning, did himself by his own coming most manifestly Consecrate the Lords day.]

And on *Col.* 2. *fol.* 308. he sheweth that the Sabbath was a shadow, and Christ that made it was Lord of it and ended it; and that to abstain from sin is now our Sabbath. See him also on *Rev.* 1. 10. *Heb.* 4. *fol.* 308. 2 *Cor.* 3. *fol.* 176. D.

And because he was a Scot, I will adde *Sedulius* who lived 430. In Col. 2. fol. 91. [*The Sabbath being a shadow ceased when the Body came, because the Truth being present, the Image is needless. And on Heb.* 4 9. *There remaineth a Rest, that is, The Eternal Rest which the Jewish Sabbath signified.*]

See *Philastrius Heres.* 8. Abundance more of this kind I might Cite, but for making the Book tedious to those that need it not. And so much of the History, to satisfie your Objections and Mistakes.

CHAP. II.

An Answer to more Arguments for the seventh day Sabbath.

Reasons.	Answers.
1. That the Lord Jesus Christ is Jehovah, Zach. 11. 13. & 12, 4,——10. Gen. 19. 24. Act. 2. 25. compared with Psal. 16. 8, &c. *The Lord our Righteousness*, Jer. 23. 6.	1. This is no Controversie among us, meaning of Christs Divine Nature; and his person in respect thereof.
2. That the World was made by Jehovah Christ, Joh. 1. 3, 10. Heb. 1. 2, 3, 10. Col. 1. 14, 15, 16, 17. Eph. 3. 9. Psal. 102. 22, 24, 25. Heb. 3. 4. Rom. 11. 36. 1 Cor. 8. 6. Gen. 2. 4, &c.	2. Nor is this any Controversie, if meant of the second person in the eternal Trinity, not yet Incarnate, nor in the flesh Annointed (Christ.)
3. The seventh day Sabbath was instituted by Jehovah Christ, and kept by him, Gen. 2. 2, 3, 4.	3. Though this have long been doubted in the Church, some thinking it mentioned but

3, 4. *whilest man was in innocency, before the Fall*, Gen. 3. 6. *(and before any Types.)* but by Anticipation, yet I deny it not, but believe that it was Sanctified and kept from the beginning, becauſe the *Reaſon* of the Conſecration was from the beginning. But, 1. The ſecond Perſon is not called *Chriſt* before the fall, nor without reſpect to his humane Nature. 2. It is uncertain whether it was before the fall; becauſe we know not whether man fell on the ſame day in which he was Created, which is the commoneſt opinion, (though unproved) Whereupon Mr. *J. Walker* in his *Treat.* of the *Sabbath* maintaineth, that the fall and promiſe went before the Sabbath, and ſo that Gods reſt had reſpect to Chriſt promiſed, as the perfection of his works, and that the Sabbath was firſt founded on Chriſt and the promiſe. But becauſe all this is unproved Opinion, I incline to the Objectors, and the common ſenſe.

4. *The ſeventh day Sabbath was kept by Abraham*, Gen. 26. 5. *by the Iſraelites*, Exod. 5. 5. *The Law for the ſeventh day was repeated* Exod. 16. 22, 23.

4. I am of the ſame opinion; but it is uncertain; ſo far as it is uncertain whether it was inſtituted actually at firſt. But the reſt, *Ex.* 5. 5. ſeemeth plainly to referr to no Sabbath, but to the peoples neglect of their tasks, while *Moſes* kept them in hope of deliverance, and treated for them. And their tasks, with their deſire, to go into the Wilderneſs to Sacrifice, maketh it probable that *Pharaoh* never allowed them the Sabbaths reſt.

5. *The Decalogue was spoken by Jehovah Christ*, Exod. 20. 1. (*see the Assemblies lesser Catechisme on the Preamble to the Commands:*) *Because the Lord is our God, &c. Redeemer, &c. therefore we are bound to keep, &c.* Exod. 19. 3. compared with Act. 7. 38. Esa. 63. 9. Ex. 19. 17. *The Decalogue written by his Finger*, Ex. 31. 18. *On Tables of Stone*, Ex. 32. 15, 16, 19. & 34, 1, 28. *and kept by all the Prophets.*

6. *The Decalogue was confirmed by Jehovah, Christ*, Mat. 5. 17, 18, 19. Luk. 16. 17. Mat. 28. 20. Joh. 14. 15. & 15. 14. Rom 3. 31. & 7. 12. Jam. 2. 8, 12. *New Covenant*, Heb. 8. 10. 1 Joh. 3. 22, 24. 1 Joh. 5. 3. 2 Ep. Joh. 5. 6. Rev. 12. 17. & 14. 12. & 22. 14, 18. compared with Mal. 4. 4.

5. All true, and uncontroverted, with these suppositions: 1. That the Father as well as the Son gave the Decalogue: 2. That the second person was not yet Incarnate, (Christ.) 3. That the Law was given by the Ministration of Angels, who its like are called the Voice and Finger of God. 4. That God our Redeemer did variously Govern his Kingdom, by his Law and Covenant in various Editions: of which more anon.

6. Here beginneth our fundamental difference: I shall first tell you what we take for the truth, and then consider of what you alledge against it.

1. We hold that every Law is the Law of some one; some Law-maker or Soveraign power: And therefore Christ being now

now the Head over all things to the Church, *Eph.* 1. 22, 23. whatever Law is now in Being to the Church, muft needs be the Law of Chrift.

2. We hold that Chrifts Redeemed Kingdom hath been Governed by him, with variety of Adminiftrations, by various Editions of his Law or Covenant : That is, I. Univerfally to Mankind ; *viz.* 1. Before his Incarnation : which was; firft, To *Adam*, and fecondly to *Noah*, and to mankind in them both : 2. After his Incarnation. II, Particularly, to the feed of *Abraham* even the Jews as a particular Political fociety; chofen out of the World (not as the only people or Church of God on Earth, but) for peculiar extraordinary mercies as a peculiar people.

3. We believe that each of thefe Adminiftrations was fitteft for its proper time and fubject, according to the manifold Wifdom of God : But yet the Alterations were many and great, and all tended towards perfection : fo that the laft Edition of the Covenant by Chrift Incarnate and his *Holy Spirit*, much excelled all that went before, in the Kingdom of the Mediatour. And all thefe changes were made by God-Redeemer himfelf.

4. As it was the work of the Redeemer to be the Repairer of Nature, and recoverer of man to God ; fo in all the feveral Adminiftrations, the great Laws of Nature containing mans duty to God, refulting from and manifefted in our Nature as related to God, and in the *Natura rerum* or the Works of God, was ftill made the chief part of the Redeemers Law : fo that this Law

of *Nature*, whose summe is the *Love of God*, and of his *Image*, is ever the Primitive unchangeable Law; and the rest are secondary subservient Laws, either *Positive*, or *remedying*, or both. And no tittle of this shall ever cease, if nature cease not.

5. But yet there are temporary Laws of Nature, which are about Temporary things; or where the Nature of the thing it self is mutable, from whence the Natural duty doth result. As it was a duty by the then Law of Nature it self; for *Adams* Sons and Daughters to Marry [Increase and multiply] being made a natural Benediction, and the means a natural Duty. And yet now, it is incest against the Law of Nature, for Brother and Sister to Marry. So it was a Natural duty for *Adam* and *Eve* before their Fall to love each other as innocent; but not so when they ceased to be innocent: For *cessante materiâ cessat obligatio*.

6. So also some Positive Commands made to *Adam* in Innocence ceased on the fall, and sentence; (As to dress that Garden.) And some positives of the first Administrations of Grace, did cease by the supervening of a more perfect administration. As the two Symbolical or Sacramental Trees in the Garden, were no longer such to man when he was turned out; so no positive Ordinance of Grace, was any longer in force, when God himself repealed it, by the introduction of a more perfect Administration.

7. Accordingly we hold, that a change is now made of the sanctified day. Where note, 1. That we take not the *seventh day*, (no nor one day in seven,

seven, though that be nothing to our Controverſie) to be a Duty by the proper Law of Nature, but by a Poſitive Law: 2. That the ſeventh day is never called a *Sabbath* till *Moſes* time, but only a *Sanctified and bleſſed day*; the word *Sabbath* being ever taken in Scripture for a day of *Ceremonial Reſt*, as well as of ſpiritual Reſt and Worſhip. 3. That Chriſt himſelf hath continued a ſeventh day, but changed the ſeventh day to the firſt; not as a Sabbath, that is, A day of *Ceremonial Reſt*, for he hath ended all Sabbaths as ſhadows of things that were to come, even of reſt which remained for the people of God, *Heb.* 4. 9. *Col.* 2. 16. And this is it which is incumbent upon us to prove, and I think I have fully proved already. 4. That having proved the thing done (the poſitive Law of the ſeventh day changed by the Holy Ghoſt to the firſt day) it concerneth us not much to give the reaſons of Gods doings: But yet this reaſon may ſecondarily be obſerved: That God having made the whole frame of Nature *very good*, did thereby make it the glaſs in which he was to be ſeen by man, and the Book which he would have man chiefly ſtudy, for the knowledge of his Maker and his Will. But ſin having introduced, diſorder, confuſion and a curſe upon part of the Creation for mans ſake, God purpoſed at once, both to notifie to man, what he had done by ſin, in bringing diſorder and a curſe upon the Creature, and blotting the Book of Nature which he ſhould have chiefly uſed, and alſo that it was his good pleaſure to ſet up a clearer Glaſs, even *Chriſt Incarnate*, in which man might ſee his Makers face, in a repreſentation

sentation suitable to our need; not now as *smileing upon* an *Innocent* man, nor as *frowning* on a *guilty man*, but as *reconciled* to *Redeemed* man; and to Write a Book in which his will should be more plainly read, than in the blotted Book of Nature: Yea in which he that in the Creature appeared most eminently in *Power*, might now appear most eminently in LOVE, even redeeming, reconciling, adopting, justifying and saving Love. So that, though God did not change the day, till the Person of the Incarnate Mediator, with his perfect last edition of the Covenant, was exhibited, and set up as this clearer Glass and Book, yet then as the seasonable time of Reformation (*Heb.* 9, 10, 11.) he did it. To teach man that though still he must honour God as the Creator, and know him in the Glass and Book of the *Creature*, yet that must be now but his secondary study; for he must primarily study God *in Christ*; where he is revealed in *Love*, even most conspicuous, wonderous Love.

And how suitable this is to man after sin and curse and wrath, may thus evidently appear.

1. We were so *Dead* in sin, and utterly deprived of the spiritual *Life*, that the Book of the Creatures, was not a sufficient means of our reviving: But as we must have the QUICKNING SPIRIT of Jesus the Mediator, so we must have a *suitable means* for that Spirit to work by: which that the cursed mortified Creature is not, appeareth in the experience of the case of Heathens

2. We were so *Dark* in sin, that the *Creature* was not a sufficient means of our *Illumination*:

But

But as we must have the ILLUMINATING SPIRIT of Jesus, so we must have a Glass and Book that was suited to that illuminating work.

3. We were so *alienated* from God, by *Enmity* and *malignity*, and loss of LOVE, that as it must be the *spirit* of Jesus which must regenerate us unto LOVE, so it must be a clearer demonstration of LOVE than the Creature maketh in its cursed state, which must be the fit means for the spirit to work by in the restitution of our LOVE.

Where further note, 1. That LOVE is *Holiness* and *Happiness* it self: and the operations of Divine *Love* are his *Perfective operations*, and so fit for the last perfective act. 2. That man had many wayes fallen from LOVE: As he had actually and habitually turned away his own heart from God; and as he had fallen under Gods wrath, and so lost those fullest emanations of Gods Love, which should cherish *his own Love* to God; and as he had forfeited the assistance of the *spirit* which should repair it; and as he was fallen in Love with the accursed Creature, and lastly as he was under the Curse or threatning himself, and the penalties begun; It being impossible to Humane Nature, to Love a God who we think will damn us, and feel doth punish us in order thereunto. So that nothing could be more suitable to Lapsed man, or more perfective of the *Appearance* and *Operations* of God, than this demonstration of Reconciling saving Love, in our Incarnate Crucified, Raised, Glorified, Interceding Redeemer. All which sheweth

sheweth that Gods removal of the *sanctified day* from the seventh to the first of the Week, and his preferring the Commemoration of Redemption, and our use of the *Glass* and *Book* of an Incarnate Saviour before that of the now accursed Creature, is a work of the admirable wisdom of God, and exceeding suitable to the nature of the things.

II. Now I come to consider of what you say against all this. You Cite the numbers of many Chapters and Verses (contrary to your *grand principles*, these *divisions* being *Humane Inventions*;) in all which there is nothing about the Controversie in hand. The Texts speak not of the *Decalogue only*, but of *the Law*, and of *Gods Commandments*, and *Chrifts Commandments*. Now I must tell you before-hand, that I will take no mans word for the Word of God, nor believe any thing that you say, *God speaketh*; without proof. Prove it, or it goeth for nothing with me. For as I know that adding to Gods Word is Cursed, Rev. 22. 18 as well as taking away; so if I must once come to believe that God saith this or that without proof, I shall never know whom to believe: For twenty men may tell me twenty several tales, and say that God saith them all.

I expect your proof then of one of these two assertions (for which it is that you hold, no man can gather by your own words, or citations.)
1. That all the Law which was in being at Chrifts Incarnation, was confirmed and continued by him (which yet I do not Imagine you to hold, because all *Pauls* Epistles, and especially the
Ep.

Ep. to the *Heb.* do so fully plead against it.) 2. Or else that by the *Law* in all those *Texts* is meant *all the Decalogue,* and the *Decalogue alone.*

The Texts cited by you prove no more than what we hold as confidently as you: *viz,* 1. That all the Law of Nature, (where the *Matter* or *Nature* of the things continue) is continued by Christ, and is his principal Law. 2. That the Decalogue as to that matter of it, is continued as it is the Law of Nature (which is almost all that is in it,) but not as the Jewish Law given by *Moses* hands to the Political body. 3. That the Natural part of all the rest of *Moses* Law is continued as well as the Decalogue. 4. That all *Moses* Law as well as the Decalogue shall be fullfilled, and Heaven and Earth shall sooner pass away than one jot or tittle of it shall pass till it be fulfilled. 5. That the Elements, Shadows, Predictions, Preparations, *&c.* are all fulfilled by the coming of Christ, and by a more perfect Administration. For Christ fulfilled all Righteousness, *Mat.* 3. 15. (δικαιοσύνη is sometimes put materially for δικαιώματα,) 6. That a *change* may be two waies made, 1. By *destroying* a thing. 2. By *perfecting* it. And that by the Law in *Matth.* 5. 17, *&c.* Christ meaneth, *the whole body of Gods Law then in force to the Jews,* considered as *one frame, consisting of Natural and Positive parts.* Of which he saith, that he came not καταλῦσαι τὸν νόμον, to dissolve, pull in pieces or destroy the Law, as a licentious Teacher, that would take off Gods obligations, and leave the Wills and Lusts of men to a Lawless liberty (which was it that the Pharises imputed to such as were against the Law;)

Law:) But that he came to bring in a *greater strictness*, a *righteousness* not only *exceeding* that of his accusers, *v.* 20. but instead of destroying it, to perfect the Law it self, that is, to bring in a perfecter Administration and Edition of the Law. So that as Generation turneth *semen in suppositum*, and so doth do away the *seed*, not by destroying it, but by changing it into a perfecter being; and as *Paul* saith, 1 Cor. 13. 16, 17, 18. *When that which is perfect is come, then that which is in part shall be done away: When I was a child, I spake as a child; I understood* (or was affected) *as a child, I thought* (or reasoned) *as a child; but when I became a man I put away childish things,* &c. not that the *child* or his *knowledge* is *destroyed*, but *perfected*, and *changed* into better; And yet many Acts of his childish reasonings may cease; And as he that would repair the Temple to a greater glory, may take away the brass, and put Gold instead of it, and so not change one pin of the Temple by a *destructive change* but by a *perfecting change*, which (to the frame) is to *edifie*, and not to *destroy*; Even so Christ professeth that he came not to gratifie the lusts of men, nor to destroy the Law in the smallest point, but 1. Himself to fulfill it in the very letter, and 2. To accomplish the shadows, Predictions and Types, by coming himself as the *Truth* and *End*, which when they had attained they were fulfilled; And 3. By a more perfect Edition and spiritual Administration, advancing the Law to a higher degree of excellency; by which not *the Law* is said to be *put away*, or *destroyed*, but the *imperfections* or weaknesses of it to be done away.

away. Not but that *all Gods Laws* are *perfect* as to the *time* and *subject* which they are fitted to; but not in comparison of the *future time*, and *degrees* to be added. It is a *Better Testament* that Christ bringeth in ; Heb. 7. 22. & 8. 6. *established on better promises*, and *procured* by *better Sacrifice*, and *bringing a better hope*, Heb. 8. 6. & 7. 19. and *better things that are provided for us, that they without us should not be made perfect*, Heb. 11. 40. So that when *Moses* Law is considered as such, in that Imperfect state, it is essentially or *formally* all done away; but not *materially*; for it is done away but by changing it into a better Testament and more perfect administration, which retaineth all that is *natural* in it, and addeth *better positives* suited to riper times.

So that the *Law* as denominated from the nobler Natural part, and as signifying the whole Law or systeme of precepts, then in force, is not destroyed, but perfected ; But the *Law* as signifying that called *Jewish* delivered by *Moses* to that Republick, as such, though part of the said systeme, yet is the Imperfect part, and is taken down and is now no Law, though it be not destroyed, but *fulfilled*, and turned into a more perfect Testament and Administration.

Now that by the *Law* and *Commandments* I am not to understand the *Decalogue only*, in any of your cited Texts, I thus prove.

1. From the *notation of the name*. The word [*Law*] in its usual proper sense, doth signifie the whole, or other parts as well as that ; and not that one part only. Therefore I must

so take it, till you prove that in any Text it hath a limited sense. Else I shall turn Gods universal or indefinite terms into particular, and pervert his word, by limiting by my own invention where God hath not limited.

2. Because the common sense in which the Jewes, (against whom Christ spake) did take the word [Law] Was not for the Decalogue only but for the *Pentateuch*, or all *Moses* Law. And if Christ speak to them, he is to be supposed to speak intelligibly, and therefore in their sense.

3. Because Christ in this very Chapter, *Mat.* 5. extendeth the sense further than the Decalogue: As *v.* 17. he adjoynes the Prophets equally with the Law, which he came not to destroy. And thus he speaketh as the Jews, who distributed the Old Testament into the *Law and Prophets*, when by the Law they meant the *Pentateuch*. Now it is certain that all the Prophesies that say [*The Messiah is not yet come, but shall come, and be incarnate*, and that shew the time and manner,] *&c.* are not now true *de futuro*, as they then spake; And yet they are not *destroyed* but *fulfilled*, and so cease as prophecies of things yet future. And so it is with the Positives of *Moses* Law. 2. *V.* 18. he saith universaly, *Till all be fulfilled*, and not the Decalogue only. 3. *V.* 19. he extendeth it to the Least command. 4. *V.* 20. he extendeth it to all the Pharises Righteousness, which was Righteousness indeed. 5. *V.* 21. [*Whosoever shall kill, shall be in danger of the Judgement,*] hath the political penalty in it, above the bare sixth Commandment. 6. *V.* 31. *Whosoever shall put away his Wife, let him give her a writing of*

of divorcement, is not the bare seventh Commandment, but fetcht from *Deut.* 24. 1. And this instance it self expoundeth, *v.* 17, 18. For when Christ had protested against destroying an *iota* or *tittle* of the Law, yet he changeth this very Law now cited by himself, so far as it indulgeth putting away; so that it is hence evident that he meaneth not that he came not to make a *perfective change*, but that he came not to indulge licentiousness, and Lust by a destructive change. *Luk.* 16. 18. 1 *Cor.* 7. 10. *Mat.* 19. 9. So 7. *V.* 33. *Thou shalt not forswear thy self*, &c. is fetcht from *Lev.* 19. 12, &c. 8. *V.* 38. *An eye for an eye*, &c. is fetcht from *Exod.* 21. 24. *Lev.* 24. 20. *Deut.* 19. 21. and not from the Decalogue alone. 9. So *V.* 43. is from *Lev.* 19. 18. and other places.

4. Because in all *Pauls* Epistles, and commonly in all the New Testament the word *Law* is *ordinarily*, if not alwayes, taken more extensively than the *Decalogue*: Therefore to expound it for the Decalogue only, is to contradict the constant use of the Scripture, under pretense of expounding the Scripture.

If then by the *Law*, be meant either the whole systeme of God's Laws, Natural and Positive, or all *Moses* Law, or the *Pentateuch*, then I may thus argue. *It is most certain that much of this Law of Moses is ceased or abrogate. Therefore it is certain, that it was none of Christs meaning that he would abrogate none of that Law which he speaketh of, or change it for a better.*

That all and every word of the Decalogue is not of the dureable Law of *Nature*, I shall prove anon.

O That

That by the word [*Law*] the Scripture meaneth more than the meer Decalogue these Texts among others prove, *Exod.* 13. 9. & 24. 12. *Deut.* 1. 5. & 4. 8. & 17. 18, 19. & 28. 61. & 29. 29. & 31. 9. 2 *King.* 17. 37. & 23. 24, 25. 2 *Chron.* 31. 21. & 33. 18. & 34. 19. *Ezra* 7. 6. & 14. 26. & 10. 3. *Neh.* 8. 2, 7, 9, 13, 14. & 10. 29. & 13. 3. *Mal.* 2. 6, 7, 8, 9. & 4. 4. *Matth.* 11. 13. & 12. 5. & 26. 36, 40. & 23. 23. *Luk.* 2. 22, 27. *Joh.* 1. 17, 45. & 7. 19, 23, 51. & 8. 5. & 10. 34. & 12. 34. & 15. 25. *Act.* 6. 13. & 13. 15, 39. & 15. 5, 24. & 21. 20, 28. & 22. 3, 12. & 23. 3, 29. & 28. 23. *Rom.* 2. 12, 13, 14, 17, 18, 20, 23. & 3. 19, 20, 21, 28, 31. & 4. 13, 14, 15, 16. & 5. 13. & 7. 1, 2, 3, 4, 5, 6, &c. And so to the end of the New Testament; which I need not further number.

7. *That the seventh day Sabbath was kept by the Lord Jehovah Christ during his life,* Mark. 1. 21. & 6. 2. *Luk.* 4. 31. & 6. 6. 1. 5. & 13. 10. *Mat.* 12. 1, 9. & 13. 1, 2. *and constantly,* Luk. 4. 16. 17. *See Christs counsel which was to come to pass about forty years after his death.* Mat. 24. 20.

7. 1. So Christ was Circumcised, and joyned in the Synagogue Worship, and held Communion with the Jewish Church, and Priesthood, and observed all the Law of *Moses,* never violating any part; For he was *made, under the Law* to redeem them that were under the Law, Gal. 4. 4, 5. Do you think that all this is established for us? 2. And his Counsel, *Mat.* 24. 20. had respect to the Jews misery and not to their *duty.* He therefore

therefore foretelleth their destruction, because they would reject him and his Law, in a perverse zeal for *Moses* Law; And therefore intimateth that even *Moses* should condemn them, and their misery should be increased by their zeal for his Law; For their City was taken on the Sabbath day, which increased their Calamity, who scrupled on that day to fight or fly. And can you think Christ approved of that opinion, who had so oft before condemned the like, about their over rigid sabbatizing? Or as Dr. *Hammond* thinks, it is liker to be spoken of a Sabbath year, when the War and Famine would come together. However it be, it only *supposeth* their adherence to their Law and Sabbath, but *justifieth* it not at all: Though yet the total and full abrogation of the Jewish Law, was not fully declared, till, at that time of the destruction of their City and Temple, their policy more fully ceased.

8. *That after Jehovah had finished the work of Redemption,* John 19 30. *his body rested in the Grave,* Mat. 27. 66. *and himself in Heaven,* Luk. 23. 42, 43. *as he rested when he ended the work of Creation,* Gen. 2. 2, 4.

8. You again adde to the Word of God: It is not said that *he had finished the work of Redemption*. But only [*It is finished*] which seemeth to mean but that, 1. This was the last act of his life, in which he was actively to fulfill the Law and offer himself a Sacrifice for man; 2. And in which all the Law and Prophets were fulfilled, which foretold this Sacrifice. For that it is not meant of the whole work of Redemption as finished

finished when he spoke these words, is evident, 1. Because after those words he was to die; 2. Because his state in death and his burial were part of his humiliation as is implyed, 1 *Cor.* 15. 4. *Joh.* 1. 7. *Rom.* 6. 4. *Col.* 2. 12. *Isa.* 53. 9. 1 *Cor.* 15. 35. *Act.* 2. 24. 1 *Cor.* 15. 26. *Phil.* 3. 10. 2 *Tim.* 1. 10. *Heb.* 2. 14, 15. 3. Because his Resurrection was his victorious act, and a part of the work of mans Redemption; 4. And so is his Intercession. For Redemption is larger than Humiliation or Sacrifice for sin. As *Exod.* 6 6. *Luk.* 24. 21. *Rom.* 3. 24. & 8. 23. 1 *Cor.* 1. 30. *Eph.* 1. 14. *Luk.* 21. 28. It is the Resurrection by which we are made Righteous and receive our hope of life, and victory over death and Satan, *Rom.* 1. 4. *Phil.* 3. 10, 11. 1 *Pet.* 1. 3. & 3. 21. *Rom.* 4. 25.

2. The clean contrary therefore to your Collection is true: *viz.* That God did indeed end the Work of his Creation on the sixth day, and rested in it, as finished on the seventh: But Christ was so far from ending his on the sixth, and resting in it on the seventh, that on that day above all other he seemed conquered by men, and by him that had the power of death, *Heb.* 2. 14. and was held as Captive by the Grave, so that his Disciples hopes did seem dead with him, *Luk.* 24. 21. This State of Death being not the least, if not the lowest part of his Humiliation: Whence came the Churches Article that he descended into *Hades.* 3. I did more probably before prove from Christs own words compared with his burial, a casting down of the seventh day Sabbath, thus. That day on which

the

peareth from *Mark.* 2. 20. When the Bridegroom is taken from them, then they shall fast. Now though this meant not to command any one day for fasting, much less the whole time of his bodily absence, yet both the sense of the words themselves, and the interpretation of the Event tell us, that as there was no day in which he was so sadly taken from them as that Sabbath day, which almost broke their hearts and hopes, (for the next day he was restored to them) So there was no day in which they were so dejected, and unlike to the Celebraters of a Gospel day of Joy, or Sabbath. Do you call the day of Satans power, and triumph, and of the Disciples greatest fear and grief that ever befell them, the Celebration of a Sabbath rest? It had indeed somewhat like an *outward* Rest, but so as seemed plainly to burie in his Grave the seventh day Ceremonial Sabbath. And from the Reasons now pleaded it was that the Western Churches kept the seventh day as a Fast.

9. Whilest the Lord Jehovah Christ rested, private believers rested according to the Commandment, Luk. 23. 55, 56. Mar. 15. 42. & 16. 1. compared.

9 A. They did indeed keep yet the Jewish Sabbath, till Chrifts Resurrection, and the coming down of the Holy Ghost : And so they did the rest of the Jewish Law. For they yet knew not that it was abrogated ; But must

we do so too? You may as well argue from their keeping the Sabbath before Christs Death, as on that day when he was dead. The change of the day was made by Degrees, by three several acts or means. 1. The Resurrection of Christ, was the *founding* act, which gave the Cause of changing it; Like Gods finishing his works of Creation at first. 2. The Inspiration of the Holy Ghost in the Apostles doth teach them, and bring all things to their remembrance which Christ commanded, and was the authorising means of the change: And the Apostles actual settlement thereupon was the Promulgation. 3. The gradual notification by the Preachers to the Churches, and finally the destruction of the Jewish Policie, and Temple, and Priesthood, were the fuller proclamation of it, and the way of bringing the change that was made by Command into fuller Execution.

10. *The seventh day Sabbath was observed by the Apostles after the Resurrection and Ascension,* Act. 13. 14, 15, 16, 42, 44. & 16. 13, 14. *And constantly,* Act. 17. 2. (*the same Greek phrase with that* Luk. 14. 16. *for Christs constant keeping the seventh day Sabbath as before*) Act. 18. 1, 4. &c.

10 A. 1. But withal, in this time they stablished the Lords day, as soon as (on that day) the Holy Ghost came down upon them.

2. So all that while they kept other parts of the Jewish Law: They scrupled, yea refused a while Communion with the Gentiles as Act. 10. shews. They so carryed it to the Jews that *Paul* made it his defence, that he had not

not offended any thing at all, either against the Law of the *Jews* or against the Temple, Act. 25. 8. And when he *Circumcised Timothy, purified himself, shaved his head,* for his Vow, *&c.* Do you think that all these are duties to Believers?

3. None of the Texts cited by you do prove that the Apostles kept the Sabbath at all *as a Sabbath,* that is, a day on which it was *their duty to Rest*; But only that they *Preached* on that day in the *Synagogues,* and to the people; For when should they Preach to them but when they were Congregated, and capable of hearing? They took it for no sin to Preach on the Sabbath no more than I would do to Preach Christ on *Friday,* which is their Sabbath, to the Turks, if they would hear me. But Sabbatizing according to the Law, was something else than Preaching.

4. And it is most evident that for a long time the Christian Jews did still keep the Law of *Moses:* And that all that the Apostles did against it then, was, but 1. To declare that Christ was the end of the Law, and so to declare the keeping of it to be *unnecessary* to Salvation, but not *unlawful,* laying by the opinion of necessity. 2. That the Gentile Christians should not be brought to use it, because it was unnecessary. For the Apostles *Act.* 15. do not *forbid* it to the *Jews,* but only to the *Gentiles,* (who were never under it.) Therefore the Apostles who lived among the Jews no doubt did so far comply with them to win them, as to keep the Law externally, though not as a *necessary thing,* that is, not as a *Law in force* obliging them, but as a thing yet lawful to further the Gospel; And therefore

therefore no wonder if *Peter* went so far as to withdraw from the Gentiles when the Jews were present, when even *Paul* the Apostle of the Gentiles who speaketh so much more than all the rest against the Law, doth yet as aforesaid Circumcise *Timothy*, shave his head, purifie himself, &c. and as he became all things to all men, so to the Jews he became a Jew. But when the Jews Policie and Temple ceased, the change was executively yet further made, and the Jewish Christians themselves were weaned from their Law. In the mean time *Paul* and *John*, *Rev.* 2. & 3. do openly rebuke the Judaizing Hereticks, the *Ebionites* and *Cerinthians*, and *Nicolaitans*, and shew the perniciousness of their conceits.

11. *The Holy Spirit call's the seventh day (and no other day) the Sabbath, throughout the Scriptures, before and after the Death, Resurrection and Ascension of the Lord Jehovah Christ,* Gen. 2. 2, 3, 4. Exod. 20. 10, &c. Act. 13. 14, 15, 16, 42, 44. & 16. 13, 14. & 17. 2. & 18. 1, 4.

11. *A.* Though it be not true that the seventh is called the Sabbath, *Gen.* 2. and though others deny the sufficiency of your enumeration, yet I grant your assertion as true. And therefore am satisfied that it is the seventh day which is put down, when Sabbatizing was put down; and that it could be none but the seventh day which *Paul* meant, Col. 2. 16. *Let no man judge you in meats,* &c. *and Sabbaths which were Shadows of things to come.* For the first day is never called a *Sabbath* as you truly say; therefore it was not put down with the Sabbath.

Sabbath.   See Dr. *Youngs Dies Dom.* on *Col.* 2. 16.

12. *The seventh day Sabbath was prophaned by the Church heretofore and reformed:* Neh. 10. 28, 29, 31. & 13. 15, 17, 18, 22. See *Belg. Annot.* on *Dan.* 7. 25, &c. *as prophesied who would change it.*

12. This is all granted. Sacrificing also was then Prophaned and Reformed, and polluted and destroyed by *Antiochus*; And yet we are not still under the obligation of Sacrificing. We are not under the Law, but under Grace.

CHAP.

CHAP. III.

Whether the seventh day Sabbath be part of the Law of Nature; or only a Positive Law?

IT is but few that I have any Controverſie with on this point: But yet one there is, who objecteth and argueth as followeth.

God hath put this into nature, Ex. 20. 10. Thy Stranger. Deut. 5. 14. *The three firſt Chapters of* Romans. *Particularly* Chap. 2. 14, 15, 26, 27. & 3. 9. 21. 1 Cor. 11. 14. *Nature hath its teachings.* *The humane Nature in the firſt* Adam *was made and framed to the perfection of the ten words; ſome Notions whereof are ſtill retained, even in the corrupt ſtate of fallen man.* Gen. 1. 26, 27. Eccl. 7. 29. Eph. 4. 20. Col. 3. 10. *The Law of the ſeventh day Sabbath was given before the ten words were proclaimed at* Sinai, Exod. 16. 23. *Even from the Creation.* Gen. 2. 2, 3. *Given to* Adam *in reſpect of his humane nature, and in him to all the world of humane creatures*, Gen. 1. 14. Pſalm 104. 19. Lev. 10. 23. Numb. 28. 2, 9, 10. *'Tis the ſame word in the Original.* *Set times of Divine appointment for ſolemn aſſembling, and for* Gods *inſtituted ſervice are directed to and pointed at, by thoſe great Lights which the Creator hath ſet up in the Heavens,* Pſal. 19. *with* Rom. 10. 4, 5, 6, 7, 8, 18, 19, 20. Deut. 30. 10, 15. John 1. 9. *Every man hath a Light and Law of Nature which he carrieth about him, and is born and bred together with him:*

him: *These seeds of truth and light, though they will not justifie in the sight of God, and bring a soul throughly and safely home to glory*, Rom. 1. 20. *Yet there are even since Adams fall, those reliques and dark Letters of this holy Law of the ten words, to preserve the memory of our first created dignity, and for some other ends, though these seeds are utterly corrupted now,* Titus 1. 15. *Natural reason will tell men, that seeing all men in all Nations, do measure their Time by Weeks, and their Weeks by seven dayes, they should (besides what of their time they offer up as due to God every day) give one whole day of every Week to their Maker, who hath allowed them so liberal a portion of time, wherein to provide for themselves and their families. There being no other proportion of time that can so well provide for the necessities of families, as six dayes of every Week, and that is so well fitted to all Functions, Callings and Employments. And the light of Nature (when cleared up) will tell men, that all labour and motion being in order to rest, and rest being the perfection and end of labour, into which labour work and motion doth pass, that therefore the seventh day which is the last day in every Week is the fittest and properest day for a religious rest unto the Creator, for his Worship,* Gen. 2. 1, &c. Exod. 20. 9. Deut. 5. 13, 14. Heb. 4. 1. 11. Exod. 31. 17. Rom. 14. 13. Exod. 23. 12. & 34. 21.

Answ. How far a day is of Natural due, I have shewed before: In all the words of this reason (which I set down as I received them) there is much which is no matter of Controversie betwen us; As that there is a Light and

and Law of Nature (which few men doubt of, who are worthy to be called men) And that by this Law of Nature God should be solemnly worshipped, and that at a set or separated time. I hope the Reader will not expect that I weary him with examining the Texts which prove this before it is denyed. But the thing denyed by us is, that *the seventh day Sabbath as the seventh, is of Natural Obligation.* The proofs which are brought for this I must examine: For indeed this is the very hindge of all our Controversie: For if this be once proved, we shall easily confess that it is not abrogate: For Christ came not to abrogate any of the Law of Nature (though as I have said, such particles of it may cease, whose Matter ceaseth, by a change in Nature it self.)

The first proof is *Exod.* 20. 10. *The stranger.* To which I answer, Our question is not Whether the Sabbath was to be rested on by Strangers that are among the Jews, but, Whether it was part of the Law of Nature? If it be intended that [*whatever such strangers were bound to, was of the Law of Nature: But strangers were bound to keep the Sabbath———Ergo———*] I deny the Major, which they offer not to prove: And I do more than deny it: I disprove it by the Instances of *Exod.* 12. 19. Was eating leavened bread forbidden by the Law of Nature? V. 48. 49. *One Law shall be to him that is home-born, and to the stranger that sojourneth among you*: Circumcision was not of the Law of Nature. *Lev.* 16. 29. Resting from all work on the tenth day of the seventh Moneth, was not of the Law of Nature, though made also the strangers duty. So eating

ing blood, and that which dyeth, or was torn, *Lev.* 17. 12, 15. So *Lev.* 25. 6. *Numb.* 15. 14, 15, 16, 26. 29. & 19. 10. & 35. 15. *Deut.* 31. 12. *Jos.* 8. 33, 34, 35. & 20. 9, &c.

The next pretended proof is, *Rom.* 2. 14, &c. where there is not one syllable mentioning the Decalogue as such, but only in general, *The Law*, so far as it was written in the Gentiles hearts. But where is it proved, that the *Law* or the *Decalogue* are words of the same signification, or extent; any more, than the *whole* and a *part* are? Or where is it proved, that none of the rest of the Law is written in Nature; but the Decalogue only? Or else that every word in the Decalogue it self is part of the Law of Nature, (which is the question.) I shall prove the contrary anon: In the mean time, the bare numbring of Chapters and Verses is no proof.

3. It is next said, that [*Adam was made and framed to the perfection of the ten words.*] *Answ.* Adam was made in the Image of God, before the ten words were given in stone: But so much of them as is of the Law of Nature, and had matter existent in *Adams* dayes, no doubt, was a Law to him as well as it is to us. But that's nothing to the question, Whether all things in the ten words are of Natural Obligation?

4. It is said, *that the Law of the seventh day Sabbath was given before the ten words were proclaimed in* Sinai. *Answ.* So was Circumcision; and so was sacrificing: yea, so was the Law about the dressing of the Garden of *Eden*, and about the eating or not eating of the fruit thereof, even in innocency; which yet were no parts of Natures

tures Laws, but Positives which now cease.

5. It is said, that *it was given to Adam in respect of his humane nature, and in him to all the world of humane creatures.* *Answ.* So was the Covenant of Works, or Innocency, which yet is at an end. But what *respect* is it (to his *humane nature*) that you mean. If you suppose this Proposition, [*Whatever Law is given with respect to humane nature, and to all men, is of natural and perpetual Obligation*] I deny it. The Law of Sacrifices and Oblations was given with respect to *humane nature*, that is, in order to its separation, and it was given to mankind, and yet not of natural perpetual obligation. The Law of distinguishing clean Beasts from unclean, and the Law against eating blood, were given to *Noah* and to all mankind, with respect to *humane nature*, Gen. 8. 20. & 9. 4. and yet not wholly of natural or perpetual obligation. All common Laws have some respect to humane nature. But if your meaning be, that this Law was given *in and with the Nature of Man himself, or that it is founded in, and provable by the very essentials of mans nature, or any thing permanent either in the nature of man, or the nature of the world,* I still deny it, and call for your proof. *Positives may have respect to humane Nature as obliged by them*; and yet not be written in humane nature, nor provable by any meer natural evidence.

6. It is said [*Set times of Divine appointment for solemn assembling*, &c. *are directed to by the great Lights,* &c. Psal. 19. Rom. 10, &c.] *Answ.* But the question is not of *set times* in general (that
some

some there be) But of this set time, the *seventh day* in particular. It will be long before you can fetch any cogent evidence from the Lights of Heaven for it. Nor do any of the Texts cited mention any such thing, or any thing that can tempt a man into such an opinion. It must be the *Divine appointment* and *institution* (which you mention,) that must prove our obligation to a particular day, and not any *nature* within us or without us.

7. The only appearance of a proof is at the end, that *time being measured by Weeks, and the end of the Weeks being fittest for Rest, therefore nature points us to the last day.*

Answ. But 1. You do not at all prove, that *nature teacheth all men to measure their time by Weeks.* 2. Nor is your Philosophy true, that *all motion is in order to rest.* Indeed all Labour is, that is, all the Motion of any Creature which is out of its proper place, and moveth towards it. But if you will call the *Action* of *Active natures*, such as our *souls* are, by the name of *spiritual motion*, or *Metaphysical motion*, as many do, then no doubt but cessation is as contrary to their nature, as corporal motion is to the nature of a stone. And the *Rest,* that is, the *perfection, pleasure* and *felicity of Spirits*, consisteth in their greatest activity in good ; *They rest not saying, Holy, Holy, &c.* 3. You transfer the case from a day of *Worship* to a day of *Rest*. And so make your cause worse: Because nature saith much for one stated day of *Worship* ; but not for one stated day of *Rest* from labour, further than the *Worship it self* must have a vacancy from other things. For reason can prove

prove no necessity to humane nature of Resting a whole day, any more than for a due proportioning of *Rest* unto *Labour* every day. The Rest of one hour in seven, is as much as the Rest of one Day in seven. Or if some more additional conveniences may be found for *Dayes* than *Hours*, there being no convenience without its inconvenience, this will but shew us, that the Law is well made when it is made, but not prove a *priore* that *there is* or *must be* such an universal Law. As you can never prove, that Nature teacheth men the distribution of Time by Weeks (1. It being a thing of Tradition, Custom and Consent. 2. And no man naturally knoweth it, till others tell him of it. 3. And many Nations do not so measure their time. 4. And no man can bring a Natural Reason to prove that it must be so, which they might do if it were a Law of Natural Reason) so also that every Family, or Countrey at least, should not have leave to vary their dayes of Rest, according to diversity of Riches and Poverty, Health and Sickness, Youth and Age, Peace and War, and other such cases, you cannot prove necessary by Nature alone , though you may prove it well done when it is done. 4 You cannot prove the *last day* more necessary for Rest, than the first, or any other. For there are few Countreys, where Wars, or some other necessities, have not constrained them sometimes to violate the Sabbaths Rest: which when they have done, it is as many dayes from the third day to the third, as from the seventh to the seventh. 5. If Time were naturally measured by Weeks, yet it followeth not, that Rest must be so: some

Countreys

than the Reason of a day for Bodily Rest, Nature will rather tell us, that God should have the *first day*, than the *last* ; *A Jove principium:* As God was to have the *first born*, the *first fruits, &c.* 7. If we might frame Laws for Divine Worship by such conceits of convenience, as this is of the last day in seven as fittest for Rest, and call them all the Laws of Nature, what a multitude of additions would be made, and of how great diversity? whilst every mans conceit went for Reason, and Reason for Nature; and so we should have as many Laws of Nature, as there are diversities of conceits. And yet that there is such a thing as a Law of Nature in which all Reason should agree, we doubt not. But having in vain expected your proof, that the seventh day Sabbath is the Law of Nature, or of universal natural obligation, I shall briefly prove the Negative (that it is not)

1. That which is of natural obligation may be proved by Natural Reason (that is, by Reason arguing from the nature of the thing) to be a duty. But that the seventh day must be kept holy as a Sabbath, cannot be proved from the nature of the thing. Therefore it is not of Natural obligation. He that will deny the Minor, let him instance in his natural proof.

2. That is not an universal Law of Nature, which Learned, Godly men, and the greatest number of these, yea, almost all the world, know

P no

no such thing by, and confess they cannot prove by Nature. But such is the seventh day Sabbath———*&c.* It is not I alone that know nothing of any such Law, nor am able by any Natural Evidence to prove it, but also all the Divines and other Christians that I am or ever was acquainted with: Nay, I never knew one man that could say, that he either had such a Law in his own nature (unless some one did take his conceit for a Law) nor that he could shew such a Law *in natura rerum*. And it is a strange Law of Nature, which is to be found in no ones Natures but perhaps twenty mens or very few in a whole age; nor is discerned by all the rest of the world. If you say, that few understand nature or improve their reason: I answer 1. If it be such a Law of Nature as is obliterated in almost all mankind, it is a very great argument that nature being changed, the Law is changed. How can that oblige which cannot be known? 2. Are not we *men* as well as you? Have not several Ages had as great improvers of nature as you? If *grace* must be the improver, are there, or have there been none as *gracious*? If *Learning* must be the improver, have there been none as learned? If *diligence* or *impartiality* must be the improvers of nature, have there not been many as diligent, studious and impartial as your selves? Let all rational men judge which of these is the better argument, [*I and twenty men more in the world do discern in Nature an universal obligation on mankind to keep the seventh day Sabbath: Therefore it is the Law of Nature.*] Or [*v. The world of mankind, godly and ungodly,*

learned

learned and unlearned, discern no such natural obligation, except you and the few of your mind: Therefore it is no Law of Nature.]

3. That is not like to be an Universal Law of Nature, which no one man since the Creation can be proved to have known and received as such by meer natural reasons without tradition. But no one man since the Creation can be proved to have known and received the seventh day Sabbath by meer natural reason without tradition: Therefore it is not like to be an Universal Law of Nature. If you know any man, name him and prove it; For I never read or heard of such a man.

4. If the Text mention it only as a Positive Institution, then it is not to be accounted a Law of nature. But the Text mentioneth it only as a Positive institution——As is plain, Gen. 2. 3. *God blessed the seventh day and sanctified it, because that in it he had rested from all his work, &c.* If it had been a Law of nature, it had been made in Nature, and the making of Nature would have been the making of the Law. But here are two arguments against that in the Text.

1. *Blessing* and *sanctifying* are positive acts of supernatural institution, superadded to the works of nature: They are not Divine *Creating* acts, but Divine *instituting* acts.

2. That which is blessed and sanctified, *Because God rested in it from all his works*, is not blessed and sanctified meerly by *those works* or that *Rest*: And if neither the *works* of *Nature*, nor the *Rest* of God from those *works* did sanctifie

fie it, then it is not of natural sanctification, and so not of natural obligation.

5. If the very *Reason* of the day be not of natural, but of supernatural *Revelation*, then the sanctification of the day is not of natural, but supernatural revelation and obligation. But the former is certain. For no man breathing ever did or can prove by Nature, without supernatural Revelation, that God made and finished his works in six dayes, and rested the seventh. *Aristotle* had been like to have escaped his Opinion of the worlds eternity, if he could have found out this by nature.

6. The distinction of *Weeks* is not known by nature, to be any necessary measure of our time; Therefore much less, that the seventh day of the Week must be a Sabbath. The Antecedent is sufficiently proved, in that no man can give a cogent reason for the necessity of such a measure. And because it hath been unknown to a great part of the world. The *Peruvians*, *Mexicans*, and many such others knew not the measure of Weeks. And *Heylin* noteth out of *Jos. Scaliger de Emend. Temp.* li. 3. & 4. and *Rossinus Antiq.* and *Dion*, that neither the *Chaldees*, the *Persians*, *Greeks*, nor *Romans* did of old observe Weeks; and that the *Romans* measured their times by *eights*, as the Jews did by sevens. *Hist. Sab.* P. 1. Ch. 4. p. 83, 84. And p. 78. he citeth Dr. *Bounds* own words, p. 65. Ed. 2. confessing the like, citing *Beroaldus* for it as to the *Roman* custom. Yea, he asserteth that till near the time of *Dionys. Exig. an.* 500. they divided not their time into Weeks as now. In which he must

needs

needs except the Christians, and consequently the ruling powers since *Constantine*. And if they were so unsetled through the world in their measure by Moneths, as Bishop *Usher* at large openeth in his *Dissert. de Macedonum & Asianorum Anno solari*, (see especially his *Ephemeris* in the end, where all the dayes of each Moneth are named without Weeks) the other will be no wonwonder.

I conclude therefore 1. That one day in seven, rather than in six or eight, may by *Reason* be discerned to be convenient when God hath so Instituted it: But cannot by Nature be known to be of natural universal obligation.

2. That this one day should be the *seventh*, no Light of Nature doth discover: Therefore Dr. *Bound*, Dr. *Ames*, and the generality of the Defenders of one day in seven against the Antisabbatarians, do unanimously assert it to be of Positive supernatural institution, and not any part of the Law of Nature: Though *stated dayes* at a convenient distance is of the Law of Nature.

CHAP. IV.

Whether every word in the Decalogue be of the Law of Nature? and of perpetual obligation? And whether all that was of the Law of Nature was in the Decalogue?

But the great argument to prove it the Law of Nature is, because it was part of the ten words written in stone. To which I say, that the Decalogue is an excellent summary of the Generals of the Law of Nature, as to the ends to which it was given; but that,

I. It hath more in it than the Law of Nature.

II. It hath *less* in it than the Law of Nature: And therefore was never intended for a *meer* or *perfect transcript* of the Law of Nature: but for a perfect general summary of so much of that Law as God thought meet to give the Jews by supernatural revelation, containing the chief heads of Natures Law (lest they should not be clear enough in Nature it self) with the addition of something more.

I. That the Decalogue written in stone hath more than the Law of Nature, is proved 1. By these instances; 1. That *God brought them out of the Land of Ægypt, and out the house of servants,* and that he is to be worshipped in that relation, is none of the Law of Nature, univerſally ſo called.

2. That God is merciful (and therefore reconciled) to thouſand Generations of them that Love him, notwithſtanding mans natural ſtate of ſin and miſery, and all mens actual ſin, this is of ſupernatural Grace, and not the Law of meer Nature.

3. The great difference between the wayes of Juſtice and mercy, expreſſed by the third and fourth Generation, compared to Thouſands, is more than the meer Law of Nature.

4. Thoſe Divines who take all Gods poſitive Inſtitutions of Worſhip, to be contained in the Affirmative part of the ſecond Commandment, muſt needs think that it containeth more than the Law of nature (Though I ſay not as they; but only that as a *General Law*, it obligeth us to perform them, when another Law hath inſtituted them.)

5. To reſt one day in ſeven is more than the Law of Nature.

6. To reſt the ſeventh day rather than the ſixth or firſt is more than the Law of Nature.

7. The ſtrictneſs of the Reſt, to do no manner of Work, is more than a Law of Nature.

8. That there be Man ſervants, and Maid ſervants, beſides *natural* inferiours, is not of the primitive or univerſal Law of Nature.

9. The diſtinction of the Iſraelites from ſtrangers within their Gates, was not by the Law of Nature.

10. That *Cattle* ſhould do no manner of work (as for a Dog to turn the ſpit in a wheel, or

ſuch

such like) is more than a Law of Nature.

11. That God made Heaven, and Earth in six dayes and rested the seventh, is not of Natural Revelation.

12. That this was the reason wherefore God blessed the Sabbath day aud hallowed it, is not of Natural Revelation.

13. Some will say that more Relations than Natural being meant in the fifth Commandment, maketh it more than a Law of Nature.

14. That the *Land* of *Canaan* is made their reward, is a positive respecting the Israelites only.

15. That *length of dayes* in that Land should be given by Promise, is an act of Grace, and not of Nature only.

16. That this promise of length of dayes in that Land, is made more to the Honouring of Superiours, than to the other commanded duties, is more than Natural.

2. I prove it also by the Abrogation of the Law written *in stone*, which I proved before ; If the Decalogue had been the *Only* and *Perfect* Law of Nature, it would not have been so far done away, as the Apostle saith it is (of which before.)

II. *All the Law of Nature was not in the Tables of Stone.* Here I premise these suppositions.

1. That a *General Law* alone, obligeth not to all particulars, without a Particular Law. E. g. If the second Command say, *Thou shalt perform all Gods instituted Worship*: Or, *Thou shalt Worship me,*

me, as I appoint thee? This bindeth no man to Baptism, the Lords Supper, &c. till another Law appoint them. Therefore there is not so much in the general Law alone, as is in that and the particular also.

2. All that is presupposed in a particular Law, is not part of that Law.

3. It is not so much to inferr a duty indirectly and by far fetcht Consequences, as to command it directly.

Now I prove the assertion by instances. All these following are Natural duties, and commanded also in other parts of Scripture, and yet are not in the Law of *Moses* as Written in Stone.

1. To believe that the soul is Immortal. 2. To believe that there is a Heaven where we shall be perfectly blessed in the Knowledge, Love and Fruition of God. 3. To believe that there is a Hell, or life of future punishment for all the impenitent. 4. To Love our selves, with a just and necessary Love, as such. 5. To take greatest care to save our souls, above our bodies. 6. To tame and mortifie all our fleshly lusts in order to our own Salvation. 7. To deny all bodily pleasure, profit, honour, liberty and life, for the securing of our salvation. 8. To forbear all outward acts of Gluttony, Drunkenness, Sloth, &c. as they tend to our own damnation. 9. To rejoice in persecution because of our great reward in Heaven. 10. To pray constantly, and fervently for Heaven, as the means of our obtaining it.

Let none say that *many* of these same things are commanded in order to *God*, and our *neighbour*. For I grant that the same material acts be
so

so; as they are expressions of Love to *God* and *Man*: But to do them in *Love* to our *selves* and for our own Salvation, is another principle and end, not contrary to, but necessarily conjunct with the former two: And indeed all the duties of *self-love* as such are past by (as supposed) in *Moses* Decalogue; because they are deeply written in mans Nature, and because the Law was Written as Political, for another use.

Obj. *But these are all supposed in the first Command of Loving God, and in the second Table, Thou shalt Love thy Neighbour as thy self.*

Answ. 1. These last are not the words of the Decalogue: but a part of the summary of all the Law. 2. Both Tables indeed *suppose* the *Love* of our selves, but that which is *supposed*, is not a part of them.

Obj. *But it is the Socinians that say the Old Testament speaketh of no reward or punishment but in this life.*

Answ. True: But *Camero* (*de tripl. fœd.*) and others that rightly understand the matter affirm, that, 1. The *Law of Nature* containeth future rewards and punishments in another life, 2. And so doth the Covenant of Grace made with *Adam* and all mankind in him, and renewed to *Noah*, *Abraham* and the Israelites, which by *Paul* is called The *Promise* as distinct from the *Law*. 3. But the *Law of* Moses *in its own proper Nature as such*, was only Political, and spake but of Temporal Rewards and Punishments. 4. Though yet all the faithful were bound to take the *Law* and *Promise* together, and so to have respect both to Temporal and Eternal things.
For

For the Law it self *connoted* and *supposed* things Eternal as our great concernment.

    III. *There is more of the Law of Nature in other parts of* Moses *Law, conjunct with the Decalogue, than is in the Decalogue alone.*
I will stay no longer in the proof of this, than to cite the places as you do. *Exod.* 23. 13, 32. & 22. 18, 20. *Lev.* 20. 1, 4, 6. *Deut.* 13. & 17. *Exod.* 23. 24. *Deut.* 12. & 23. *Lev.* 24. & 23. 3. *Exod.* 12. 16. *Deut.* 23. 18. *Exod.* 22. 28. & 23. 20. & 21. 15, 17. *Lev.* 19. 32. *Deut.* 21. & 1. & 16. & 6. & 11. *Exod.* 21. 12, 13, 18, 20, 22, &c. & 22. 2, 3. *Lev.* 13. 14. & 17. *Deut.* 21. *Exod.* 22. 19. *Lev.* 18. & 19. 29. & 20. *Deut.* 22. *Exod.* 21. 16, 21, 32, 35. & 22. 1. 4. to 17. *Lev.* 19. 30, 35. *Deut.* 24. & 29. 14. & 21. & 25. *Exod.* 23. 1. to 9. *Deut.* 23. & 24. *Lev.* 19. 11, 15. *Exod.* 22. 21, 22. & 25. & 26. & 23. 4. *Lev.* 19. 14, 16, 18, &c.
    By all this I shew you why, 1. I allow not of your *making* the word *Law* in the New Testament to signifie the Decalogue only, or taking them for equipollent terms. 2. Why I take not the *Decalogue* and the *Law* of *Nature*, for equipollent termes, or their matter to be of the same extent: And consequently why I take it for no proof that all things in the Decalogue are perpetual, because all things in the *Law* of *Nature* are so.

                                     CHAP.

CHAP. V.

Whether the truest Antiquity be for the seventh day Sabbath as kept by the Churches of Christ?

IT is here further objected that the seventh day Sabbath hath the truest testimonies of Antiquity: that it is controvertible when and how the Lords day came in; but the Antiquity of the seventh day Sabbath is past Controversie: that the Eastern Christians long observed it, and Antichrist in the West did turn it into a Fast: that the Empire of Abassia keepeth it to this day.

Answ. There is enough said of this before, were it not that some Objectors causlesly look for more. I answer therefore, 1. That it is true that the Sabbath is more ancient than the Lords day; And so is *Moses* more ancient than Christ Incarnate, and his Law than the Gospel as delivered by Christ and his Apostles, and Circumcision than Baptism, and the Passover than the Lords Supper; And so every mans Conception, Nativity, Infancie and Ignorance was before his Maturity and Knowledge. And what can you gather from all this? Thus the Papists say that their way of Religion was in *England* before ours, and that the reliques of it

in

is ever after the difeafe : Though
hey fpeak of our Religion it felf ;
ere before their errours, as Health is
fs.   But they fhould confider, that
gative the Heathens excell us both :
y may fay, you have yet many Mo-
our more ancient Religion, which
t been able to obliterate: You ftill
Veek dayes by our ancient names,
nday, &c. Your adoration towards
 fetcht from us, and fo were abun-
ur Cuftomes : Which we hope may
reputation of our Religion.

 fhewed you already how and why
 Chriftians kept the Sabbath :
pt it not as a Sabbath, but only met
 as they did on the fourth and the
, (*Wednefdayes* and *Fridayes*) as it
England to this day. And for the
ey Celebrated not the *Lords* Supper on
And they abhorred the keeping it as
eft.

met on that day for all thefe Reafons.
having been ufed in the beginning to
day in the Week (when they had all
mon, and were to fhew the power of
elical Doctrine to the height, *Act.* 2.
. & 4. 33, 34, 35.) as they found
etrive their community, fo did they
eldomer, and yet not fo feldome as
once

once a Week: And therefore as we now keep other meetings for Lectures and Prayers, besides the Lords day, so did they then on *Wednesdayes, Fridayes,* and *Saturdayes.* 2. Because the Conversion of the Jews was a great part of their work and hope: And therefore to win them, they would with *Paul* become Jews, that is, not affect an unnecessary distance, but come as neer them as Lawfully they could. 3. Because Converted Jews were no small part of the Eastern Churches: who could not easily be quite brought off from Jewish Customes; And the rest were unwilling to offend them, being taught not to despise the weak that observed meats and dayes, *Rom.* 14. & 15. *Gal.* 2. 4. Because the Assemblies on the seventh day were taken as fit preparatories to the sanctifying of the Lords day, on which account the Church of *England* now appointeth them. These things one that is acquainted with Church History needeth no proof of.

And they are sufficiently proved before. *Ignatius* words before cited are full. And those of the Council of *Laodicea, Can.* 29. are more full, who do at once appoint meetings on the seventh day, and yet Anathematize them that Judaize thereon, by bodily rest; and would have men labour on it, and preferr the Lords day before it.

Justin Martyr in his Dialogue with *Trypho,* doth largely shew that Circumcision and the Sabbath are ceased by the coming of Christ, and his Institutions, and are not now to be used by Christians. And what writer have we of full reputation

reputation and credibility more ancient than *Justin*, from whom any testimony in this case might be sought?

Tertullian (one of the next) *li. 2.* against *Marcion* saith, that the Sabbath was for that Time, and present occasion, or use, and not for perpetuity.

Athanasius was one that was for meeting on the Sabbath: And yet writeth his Book *de Sab. & Circum.* purposely to prove that the Sabbath is ceased with Circumcision as a Shadow, and that now the Lords day is the sanctified day. And the like he hath most expresly *in Homil. de Sementie,* as is cited before, saying that, *The Master being come, the Usher was out of use; and the Sun being risen the Lamps are darkened.*

Basil Ep. 74. Writeth against *Apollinaris* for holding that after the Resurrection, we should keep Sabbaths, and Judaize; As if that were the perfection to which Christ would restore men.

See *Greg. Nazianz. Orat.* 43. And *Chrysost. Hom.* 19. *in Mat.* 12. against the use of the Sabbath. *Cyril. Hieros. cat.* 4. *& Epiphan.* against the *Nazarei,* condemn them for keeping the Sabbath and Circumcision, though withal they kept the Lords day. The same doth *Epiphanius li.* 1. *Her.* 30. *n.* 2. and before him *Eusebius Hist. li.* 3. say of the *Ebionites. Augustine* oft telleth us, that the observation or keeping of the seventh day Sabbath is ceased, and not to be done by Christians. *Qu. ex. N. Test.* 69. *Ad Bonif. l.* 3. *Contr. Faust. Manich. li.* 6. *c.* 4. *De Genes. ad lit. l.* 4. *c.* 13. *de Spir. & lit. c.* 14. *de util. Cred. c.* 3.

3. And

3. And as for the *Abaſſians* keeping the Sabbath, Its true, they keep that day in some sort: But it is as true, that they use Circumciſion, and many other Jewiſh Ceremonies; beſides oft Baptizings; And that they profeſs not to uſe theſe as the Jews do, but only as ancient Cuſtomes, and as *Paul* did while he complyed with them, uſing the outward action for other ends than *Judaizers* do. And the rather becauſe they think their Emperours deſcended from *Solomon*. But the Lords day they keep on the ſame account as other Chriſtians. And if this inſtance make any thing for Sabbatizing, it will make as much for Circumciſing, and other Jewiſh rites, but nothing againſt the Sanctifying of the Lords day.

4. And as for the matter of *Faſting* on the Sabbath, the Churches greatly varyed in their Cuſtomes. The *Eaſtern* Churches, and *Millan* in the *Weſt*, were againſt Faſting on the Sabbath on two accounts, 1. Becauſe, as is ſaid, they would not offend the Jewes. Even as many peaceable Non-Conformiſts, who are againſt many Holy dayes now eſtabliſhed, do yet forbear labouring and opening their Shops on thoſe dayes, becauſe they will not give offence; Yea and go to hear the Sermons on thoſe dayes, though they keep them not Holy *as ſuch* dayes. 2. Becauſe there were many ſorts of Hereticks in thoſe times, who held that the World was made by an evil God, and thence came evil, and ſo they Faſted on the ſeventh day on that reaſon: Which made the Chriſtians avoid it leſt they ſhould Symbolize with thoſe Hereticks. And therefore the (real

or

or pretended) *Ignatius* speaketh so severely against *Fasting* on the *Sabbath*, as well as on the Lords day. And so do the Constitutions called the Apostles; yea and the Canons called theirs, *Can.* 65.

But in the *Western* Churches, (as is aforesaid) both *Jews* and *Hereticks* were more distant, or less considerable for numbers; and therefore they fasted on the seventh day, and that the rather lest they should seem by Sabbatizing to Judaize. Which was before Antichrists appearing, unless you think all the holy Doctors before cited, and all the Western Churches to be Antichristian.

Having gone thus far I here add two more Scripture Arguments to prove the abolition of the Jewish Sabbath. The first is because it is frequently made (as Circumcision is) a sign of the particular Covenant between God, and that Nation as they were a political body, and peculiar people. Therefore if their Policy cease, and Gods relation to them as a Political body, and peculiar people, and so that Political Covenant with them, then also the *signe* of the Covenant and Relation ceaseth. And though the word [*for ever*] is sometime added, it is no other than is oft added also to the Jewish Law and Ceremonies.

2. From *Act.* 15. Where the case is determined by a Council of Apostles, Elders and Brethren, yea by the Holy Ghost. *V.* 28. It appeareth by *V.* 24. that the thing asserted by the false Teachers was, [that the Gentiles *must be Circumcised and keep the Law*; that is, *of Moses*] *V.* 1.

Now the seventh day Sabbath was part of that Law (As *Sacrificing* was, though it was a Law before.) But the Holy Ghost determineth the case, [*to lay on them no greater burden than these necessary things,*] after named; where the *Sabbath* is none of them, and therefore hereby shut out. The precepts given to *Noah* are named (of which the Sabbath was not one.)

Obj. *By this Exposition you may say that the rest of the Decalogue is excluded :* For Idolatry, Murder, &c. are not here forbidden by name. *Answ.* I have fully proved that the Decalogue as written in Stone, and part of the Law or Covenant of *Moses* is not at all in force, especially to the Gentiles; nor yet as part of the Covenant (or promise) of Works, made with *Adam* in Innocency : For the form of the Promissory Covenant of Works ceased upon mans sin, and the promise of a Saviour; And the *form* of the Mosaical Law or Covenant never reached to the Gentile Nations and is ceased to the Jews : Therefore the *Matter* must cease as it constituted the same Covenant, when the *forme* ceased : And *Paul* saith expresly that this Law Written in Stone is done away : But, 1. The *Law of Nature* as a meer Law never ceased : 2. And Christ hath taken it into his Covenant, as part of the Matter of it : So that it is wholly in force, though not as part of the Covenant of Works, either *Adamical* or *Mosaical*. But the Sabbath as to the seventh day, was no part of the Law of Nature, as is proved : And *Paul* expresly saith that it was a *shadow of things to come,* and is therefore vanished away, *Col.* 2. 16.

Had

Had it been part of the Law of Nature, it had bound us as such and as Chrifts Law : or had it been one of the Enumerated particulars, *Act.* 15. it had bound the Neighbour Gentiles, *pro tempore* at leaft. But being neither, that Council difchargeth Chriftians from the obfervation of it, as far as I can underftand the Text.

FINIS.

FINIS.

Postscript.

IT is long since the foregoing Treatise was promised to a Person of Honourable Rank, who was enclined to the Jewish Sabbath; but before it was finished, or well begun, I had a sight of a Treatise on the same subject, by the late Reverend Worthy Servant of Christ Mr. *Hughes* of *Plimouth*, which enclined me to take my promised work as unnecessary. But yet some reasons moved me to reassume it. Near two Moneths after it went from me to the Press, the said Treatise of Mr. *Hughes* first, and after another on the same subject by Dr.

Dr. *J. Owen* came abroad. Yet do I not reverse mine, because many Witnesses in an Age of *Enmity* and *Neglect*, can be no injury to a truth so serviceable to the Cause of Christianity, and the prosperity of the Church, and the good of souls. Though if I were one that took the Churches prosperity to consist in the Riches, Grandeur, Ease and *Domination* or Empire of Papal Pastors, rather than in the humble, holy, heavenly, self-denying imitation of a *Crucified Christ*, I would have forborn a subject which is all for our preparation for a Heavenly Sabbatism, and carrieth men above the sensual Rest of Fleshly men, and therefore is so much disrelished by them, *Rom.* 8. 6, 7, 8. But supposing it my duty to do what I have done, I think meet to advertise the Reader, that when several men treat of the same subject, though they speak the same things in the main, yet usually each of them bringeth some considerable light, which is omitted by the rest: And as the same Spirit sets them all on work, so all together give fuller evidence to the truth, than any one of them alone. And I hope the Concourse of of these three Tractates doth prognosticate, that (though the Devil hath so contrived the business for the Prophane, that like Papists, they will hear and read none, but those that are not like to change them; yet) God will awaken the sober and serious believers of this Age, to a more holy and fruitful improvement of his day; which will greatly tend to the encrease of real Godliness, and consequently to the recovery of the dying hopes of this *apostatizing* and *divided* Age.

But that which moveth me to write this *Postscript*, is to acquaint thee, for the prevention of scandal by any seeming differences in our Writings, 1. That it cannot be expected, that all who plead the same Cause, should say just the same things for it, for matter and manner of argumentation.

2. That if I own the Name *Sabbath* less than some others, and adhere more to the name of the *Lords Day*, I do not thereby oppose the use of the name of *Sabbath* absolutely; nor is that in it self a Controversie about the *Matter*, but the *Name*, which though not contemptible, yet is of far less moment than the *Thing*. 3. That

3. That if I make not use of so many Old Testament Texts as some others, I do not thereby deny the usefulness of them, nor call you off from the consideration of any argumentation or evidence thence offered you.

4. That if I seem to be more for the cessation of *Moses* Law than some others, even of that part which was written in Stone, yet no part of the Law of Nature is thereby denyed by me any more than by any of them; And they that are angry with me, for writing so much against the Antinomians, should not also be angry with me for going no further from them, than the force of Truth constraineth me.

5. That you must pardon me for my purposely avoiding the name of the [*Moral Law*] Mr. *Cawdry* and Mr. *Palmer* who have written most largely of the Sabbath, have told you the reason. I love not such *names*, as are not fitted to the nature of *things*, but are fitted to signifie almost what the Speaker pleaseth.

I know no Law which is not *formally Moral*, as being *Regula actionum Moralium*. And men may if they will, as well confine the signification of the word

word [*Law*] it self, as of a [*Moral Law*]. Nor doth *use it self* sufficiently notifie the distinguishing signification of it: For one meaneth by that name, all the Law of *Nature* as such. Another meaneth only so much of the Law of Nature as is common to all mankind. Another meaneth all Positive Laws of supernatural Revelation, which are perpetual and universal, as well as the Law of Nature. Therefore without finding fault with others, it sufficeth me to distinguish Laws by such names as plainly signifie the intended difference. And though by the *Law of Nature*, I mean not formally the same thing that some others do, I have sufficiently opened my sense and the reasons of it, in my Reasons of the Christian Religion.

6. That they who say, that the Old Covenant, or the Covenant of Works made by *Moses* with the Jews is abrogate or ceased, and the Decalogue as a part of, or belonging to that Covenant, do say the same thing that I do, when I maintain that the Decalogue and whole Law as Mosaical is ceased, but that all the *Natural part* is

by

by Christ assumed into his Law or Covenant of Grace. For it is the same thing which is denominated the *Law* (of *Moses*, or of Christ) from the preceptive part, and and a Covenant from the *terms*, or sanction, especially the Promissory part. Nor is there any part of the *Law* of *Moses*, which was not a part of the Mosaical *Covenant*. And if the *Form cease* which denominateth, the *Being* and *denomination* ceaseth, and all the *parts* as *parts* of that which ceaseth. So that if the Covenant of Works made with the Jews cease (which *Camero* calleth a third or middle Covenant, and several men do variously denominate, but the Scripture calleth *the old*, or *former Covenant*, or *Testament*, or *Disposition*) then all the Law as part of that Covenant ceaseth: And that is as much as to say also that it ceaseth as meerly Mosaical, or Political to the Jews. And then the Argument is vain, *This or that word was written in the Tables of Stone: Therefore it is of perpetual obligation.* For as it was written *in* Stone, it was Mosaical, and is done away; and under the New Covenant all that is Natural and

Con-

Creation is described by a *Cessation* from his work, with a complacency in the goodness of it: but Christs Rest is described more by Vital *Activity* and *Operation*, than by *Cessation* from *work*, even his Triumphant Resurrection as the Conquest of Death, and beginning of a New Life: so I think the Old Sabbath is more described by such *Corporeal Rest*, or Cessation *from* work, which was partly Ceremonial, or a signifying shadow, and that the word Sabbath is never used in the Scripture, but for such a day of Ceremonial Rest (though including holy Worship). But that the *Lords day* and its due observation is more described by *spiritual Activity* and *Operation*, in the spiritual Resurrection of the soul, and its new Life to God; And that the *Bodily Rest* is no longer *Ceremonial* or *shadowy*, but fitted to the promoting and subserving of the *spiritual Activity* and *Complacency* in God and holy exercises of the mind, as the *body* it self is to the service of the soul.   8. That

8. That I am not ignorant that many of the *English* Divines long ago expound *Matth.* 24. 20. of the Christian Sabbath, and *Col.* 2. 16. as exclusive of the Jewish Weekly Sabbath: But so do not most Expositors, for which I think they give very good reasons, which I will not stand here to repeat.

9. That I intended not a full and elaborate Treatise of the Lords Day, but a brief Explication of that Method of proof which I conceive most easie and convincing, and fittest for the use of doubting Christians; who are many of them lost in doubts in the multitude and obscurity of arguments from the Old Testament: when I think that the speedy and satisfactory dispatch of the Controversie is best made by a plain proof of the Institution of Christ by the Holy Ghost in the Apostles; which I thought to have shewed in two or three Sheets, but that the necessity of producing some evidence of the fact, and answering other mens Objections, drew it out to greater length. And my method required me to say more of the practice of Antiquity, than some other mens. But again,

again, I muſt give notice that Dr. *T. Youngs Dies Dominica* is the Book which I agree with in the Method and Middle way of determining this Controverſie, and which I take to be the ſtrongeſt written of it: And that I omit moſt which he hath, as taking mine but as an Appendix to his, and deſire him that will write againſt mine, to anſwer both together, or elſe I ſhall ſuppoſe his work to be undone.

FINIS.

www.ingramcontent.com/pod-product-compliance
Lightning Source LLC
Chambersburg PA
CBHW021410230426
43666CB00006B/700